MORE THAN A GAME

MORE THAN A GAME

By Joe Smalley

Campus Crusade for Christ, Inc.

San Bernardino, California 92414

MORE THAN A GAME

A Campus Crusade for Christ Book

Published by
HERE'S LIFE PUBLISHERS, INC.
P.O. Box 1576
San Bernardino, CA. 92402

Library of Congress Catalogue Card 81-82490
ISBN 0-86605-030-2
HLP Product No. 40-292-5
©Copyright 1981, Campus Crusade for Christ, Inc.

Printed in the United States of America.

TABLE OF CONTENTS

TABLE OF CONTENTS

TO MOM AND DAD

for the sacrifices you've made

for three sons

ACKNOWLEDGMENTS

Thanks to my good friend, Kathy Kaiser, for many hours at the typewriter, for encouraging words and editorial suggestions; to Bill Horlacher, whose editing and organizational recommendations proved invaluable in shaping the manuscript; and to Rev. Ken and Joy Gage for convincing me I could write a book.

Joe Smalley

FOREWORD
By Pat Williams
General Manager, Philadelphia 76ers

The high-visibility world of sports provides the Christian athlete with a unique platform for sharing his faith in Jesus Christ. Not only do his words tell of how Christ has changed his life, but his actions also show a difference — by the way he reacts to bad calls and bad breaks, by his attitude toward his opponent and by his dedication to personal excellence.

That is why organizations like Athletes in Action are so valuable. The individuals involved with AIA know what it means to use their athletic abilities to glorify God, while also encouraging and teaching other athletes to do the same.

Joe Smalley has written a compelling book in MORE THAN A GAME. The history of Athletes in Action is filled with successes and victories, as well as its share of struggles and apparent defeats. But through it all, one message comes through clearly: In the pressure and strain of competition, faith in Christ is not only relevant, it is essential. For the Christian athlete, his chosen sport really is MORE THAN A GAME.

BEATING RUSSIA WITH LOVE

*"They (Russia) have all these super-human
beings they have trained. Professionals. The
Russians use (victories) to brainwash people
that the United States is weak, that Communism is better. We are so dumb that we
don't know we lose great prestige around the
world when the Russians beat us."*

Dale Brown
Head Basketball Coach
Louisiana State University

The French crowd was on its feet sending chants of
"USA! USA! USA!" reverberating throughout the arena.

The United States, represented in the prestigious
French Christmas Classic Basketball Tournament by
the Athletes in Action (AIA) amateur squad, was,
incredibly, holding on to a three-point lead over the
awesome Soviet Union national team.

"Zone! Zone!" Assistant Coach Wardell Jeffries
could barely make himself heard as he changed AIA's
defensive alignment, at the direction of Head Coach Jim
Poteet.

The Russian team, winner of the recent European
Championships, had lost only two games in western
Europe in the previous five years. They rated a heavy
favorite today having whipped AIA in their last two
meetings.

Nobody in Paris' packed Coubertin Arena thought
the lead would last, but halftime had come and gone,
the lead remained, and precious seconds were ticking
off the clock.

AIA-USSR. It has to be the most natural rivalry in the world. Athletes in Action, a group of post-college amateurs, all evangelical Christians playing under the banner of Campus Crusade for Christ International— against the atheists, the antithesis of everything American—representing Karl Marx and Mother Russia.

The French, while enthusiastic, are generally a reserved lot at basketball games—at least by American standards. Opting for soft contemporary music like "Raindrops Keep Falling on My Head," instead of the blaring pep band variety typical at American games, the French traditionally applaud both teams in a contest. But not today. And the zealousness of the throng gathered in Coubertin Arena went far beyond mere enthusiasm.

One would think that the allied troops had just liberated Paris. But, no, that celebration took place 35 years ago. This day is December 28, 1979, a date which history already suggests could be as significant as the liberation day back in 1944.

Today an event occurred that rocked the world, perhaps permanently damaging East-West relations. This event forced nations to one side of the global fence or the other—to the Soviet bloc or to the West— in lines more definitive than at any time since World War II. The occurrence brought sanctions and embargos, and caused 40 of the world's countries to unite in a controversial boycott of the 1980 Olympics. On this day, December 28, 1979, Russian troops invaded Afghanistan.

Paris, France, is a long way from Afghanistan. And the stakes in a basketball game are a small matter next to the life-and-death consequences of war. But a certain type of war is fought on a court or playing field in which entire nations become, not physically, but emotionally involved. America's dramatic hockey win in the 1980 Winter Olympics—just 48 days after the AIA-USSR basketball game—demonstrates that fact. The gold medal gave America one of its biggest morale boosts in a decade.

The French somehow felt a stake in this basketball game. Whether an emotional bond or natural support for an ally, they felt it. The general reaction was outrage as news of the Russian invasion spread. Unlike most people around the world, the basketball fans who filed into the arena that afternoon had a means to vent their anger. The atmosphere was electric, tense. When the teams made their flag-bearing, ceremonial entrances, the Americans were cheered fervently; the Soviets met stony silence.

The people in Coubertin Arena felt more like allies than basketball fans, and now, with AIA on the verge of an incredible upset, emotions reached a feverish pitch.

With five minutes remaining, Athletes in Action held a precarious 65-62 lead. Brad Hoffman brought the ball down-court for AIA. Accelerating, he cut quickly through the lane; twisting and turning, he drove to the basket. He slipped, but maintained enough balance to flip the ball up with a twist off the backboard. A hard-earned basket, and two more points.

The announcement over French television of the absence of Russian center, Vladimir Tkachenko, a gargantuan 7-foot-5, 280-pounder, and Sergey Belov, both officers in the Red Army, caused a stir and left a void in the Soviet middle.

The Russian explanation was that both men were in the motherland to be married to their sweethearts. Speculation swirled, however, that perhaps Russia's latest military venture required their services elsewhere.

Hoffman and fellow guard Derrick Jackson exploited that emptiness with repeated drives and quick passes to AIA's big men. But the partisan crowd didn't view the five-point lead as a comfortable margin at all. They stayed on their feet, shouting: "USA! USA! USA!"

And then the Russians began to show why they perennially rank at the top of the amateur basketball world. They began to press the younger American team and stole the ball twice for easy lay-ups. A shot by AIA center Steve Schall fell just short, bouncing off the rim on another USA possession. The tide continued to turn.

Sharpshooting Soviet forward Anatoly Myshkin hit a shot from the corner and suddenly the Russians trailed by just one point, 72-71. Less than a half-minute remained.

"I knew it could not be," one Frenchman said, turning to a friend. "The Russkies will win it, you watch."

But then something out of the ordinary happened. The American team apparently didn't realize that the "script" called for them to choke, to panic, to find a way to lose.

Jackson stole the ball from Russian point guard Stanislav Eremin and began dribbling madly across the floor using up as much of the clock as possible. Fifteen seconds . . . fourteen . . . the clock was now America's ally. Two Russians closed in on Jackson; he flipped the ball over his head to teammate Tim Hall, a forward. Seven . . . six . . . "USA! USA!" Hall to Hoffman, back to Jackson. Jackson was fouled with four seconds left.

Jackson stepped to the free throw line for the first shot of a one-and-one opportunity. The outcome of the game rested with him. It was Jackson's wizardry and

Hall's consistency (20 points and 14 rebounds) that had led AIA the entire afternoon. Jackson had played the game of his life. But now, if he missed, he could still be the goat. The Soviets would have just enough time to grab a rebound and get the ball downcourt for the winning basket.

For the first time that afternoon the crowd was silent as Jackson's shot arched toward the basket. So quiet, in fact, that one could almost hear the swish of the net as the ball sailed through. The crowd roared. Jackson's teammates surrounded him, slapping his back, shaking his hand—then moved back to their positions.

The second shot was crucial, too; with a miss the Soviets could score and send the game into overtime. Jackson wiped his forehead with the back of his hand and took the ball from the referee. He bounced the ball three quick times, looked up and with barely a pause put the ball in the air. Perfect!

The Soviets got the ball downcourt as expected, but an errant shot fell short, harmlessly. Athletes in Action had won 74-71, an incredible upset! Joyful bedlam broke loose in Coubertin Arena. The AIA players joined in as the Russians stood watching in disbelief.

The Russian coaches wondered how they would explain to Moscow what had happened to them in the French Classic. They were having difficulty translating "Christian team" into Russian and finally came up with something close, but not close enough. The Kremlin sports authorities had a hard time understanding why their team had lost to a "group of priests!"

The French media heaped praise on Jackson for his part in the upset, calling him the "black jack-in-the-box" because he "kept popping up all over the place."

The contacts between the Russian and American players, which had been quite amiable before news of the invasion arrived, were more limited after the game. A KGB agent shielded the Russian players from westerners as much as possible to protect them from "ideological contamination." A KGB agent always travels with Soviet teams; sometimes he's the "trainer," sometimes he is an "assistant coach"—but he is always there.

Actually, it was only the tournament officials and perhaps the fans who showed concern for the political situation. If the players on either team were at all concerned about political ramifications they did a good job concealing it.

The Soviet players kept their sense of humor. Eremin, the point guard, and AIA's Dan Frost, a starting forward who sat out the game with a broken finger, happened to board the same elevator in the host hotel (the plush "Sofitel") after the game. "Next time, Frost," Eremin said in broken English, "if you play—we win."

Counce, Schall, and reserve forward Ron Gottschalk later visited one of the Russians' rooms on the hotel's 11th floor. A half-dozen Russian players had gathered in the room after the game. Healthy rounds of vodka had apparently dulled the sting of defeat.

"Ah, yes, our American friends," said Myshkin. The Americans entered the room . . . thanks, but no, they would pass on the vodka.

The conversation covered assorted topics—universities, American hamburgers and basketball, but no politics and *no* invasion. Mostly basketball. The Russians said they had tried to convince Tkachenko, the 7-foot-5 center, to mary Uliana Semenova, the 7-foot-2 center for the Soviet Women's National Team. "Their children will be 8-foot-2," Eremin joked, "and we will win the 1996 Olympics!"

For avowed atheists, the Russians showed a surprising interest in spiritual things. One AIA player had
given Russian Coach Alexandr Gomelsky a gospel
tract and a creation-versus-evolution booklet. All the
USSR players had been slipped Russian Bibles at one
time or another. Gomelsky even told one of his players
that if he had any questions about the Bible he ought
to see a particular player on the AIA team. The
creation-versus-evolution tracts were of special interest
to the Russians, several of whom wanted to talk
further, and did.

The Athletes in Action team proclaimed their evangelistic message to all of France through radio, TV,
and newspaper people who recorded their every move.
Never had the European media encountered a team
quite like Athletes in Action.

"Is it true that you sometimes grab the microphone
at halftime and preach?"

"Well, not exactly . . . ."

The AIA athletes did not speak during halftimes in
Europe. Nonetheless, the trip presented some of the
most significant and far-reaching ministry opportunities the team had ever enjoyed. Athletes in Action had
reached a pinnacle of success to open the new decade.

It had been an arduous climb to the top. There was
a day not so long ago when Athletes in Action
struggled, not to beat the world's finest teams, but for
credibility, to merely gain an identity. For years, it was
only by faith that AIA players could imagine athletic
achievements of any magnitude.

The essence of this team is faith. It took faith for a
man named Dave Hannah to arrange the team's first
schedule when he had one player and no coach. And it
took faithful players to recruit their own coach.

It all began during the hot July of 1966. Dave

Hannah's dream was about to come true. But first, he had to learn whose dream it really was . . . .

---

1. Dale Brown, "At Least One Coach Believes Olympic Boycott is a Blessing," *Los Angeles Times*, June 6, 1980, Part III, p. 2, col. 1.

A DREAM REDIRECTED

"I don't think you're man enough to do it."

*John Flack, Campus Crusade Field
Director, to Dave Hannah regarding
Hannah's dream of starting an athletic
ministry.*

George Allen, head coach of the Los Angeles Rams, walked to the front of the room and paced a few steps, first this way, then the other. His audience, a gathering of 50 or so draft picks and free agents, paid rapt attention.

"We might have room for two of you guys," the coach said. One free agent, seated on a bench near the front of the room, thought to himself, "Gee, I wonder who the other guy is."

The free agent, two years out of Oklahoma State, had never been drafted, never played pro football, and before now, had never tried pro football . . . uncommon confidence for *any* pro football rookie.

But for Dave Hannah, a 25-year-old punter, confidence abounded, and not just because he could boot a football far and long. Presumptuous as it may sound, Hannah was convinced that it was God's will for him to be with the L.A. Rams! He wanted to start a ministry with athletes, and what better way, he figured, than from the "inside."

Not that he planned to make the team on faith alone. Hannah had ranked among the nation's finest punters as a collegian at Oklahoma State University. His punts sometimes sailed 65 yards in the air, but he could also handle field goals and kick-offs.

"Why," he thought, "should the Rams pay two men to do the job I can do alone?"

And now, standing 6-foot-3 and having beefed himself up to 260 pounds by weight lifting, Hannah had raw force behind his kicks that a more typically-sized kicker lacked. How many NFL kickers can do half-squats with a 1260 lb. bar on their shoulders?

Hannah had chosen not to begin a football career two years before when he graduated from Oklahoma State. Despite the interest of pro scouts, Hannah was tired of football and ready to begin life with his bride, Elaine, and a new ministry with Campus Crusade for Christ—not a professional athletic career.

Like many retired athletes, Hannah soon missed his sport, however, and after a year-and-a-half as director of Campus Crusade's work at the University of Oklahoma, he began to work out again.

It was also during that winter of 1966 that the idea for a Campus Crusade athletic ministry came to Hannah.

The idea soon became a desire, the desire a plan and the plan grew until Hannah's vision encompassed an athletic organization of worldwide proportions.

Dave Hannah has never been accused of thinking too small—a pessimist he's not. "Optimist" also falls short in characterizing him. While pessimists are people who look at a glass of water and describe the glass as half empty, optimists look at the same glass and announce it's half full. And then there are the Dave Hannahs of the world who say, "Let's add some ice cubes, some cherry Kool-Aid and some drinking

Dave, Eric, Elaine, and Scott Hannah. Dave's family comes second only to relationship with God.

AIA's John Peterson receives gold medal at Montreal Olympics in 1976. Peterson was America's only wrestling gold medalist that year, finishing his stellar mat career with a perfect 67-0 dual meet record with AIA.

Former AIA gymnast Alan Heller directed gymnastics program after retirement from active competition.

Hoffman brings the ball downcourt in the face of an opponent in first Coaches' All-American game in 1978.

straws and make something out of this thing!" People
like Hannah are called visionaries, and they're dan-
gerous in a nice sort of way. They make things
happen.

Hannah was ready to make an athletic ministry
happen and he wasted no time in sharing his vision for
a Campus Crusade for Christ athletic outreach with
Dr. Bill Bright, Campus Crusade's founder and
president.

"I'm delighted to hear that, Dave," was Dr.
Bright's response. "I've been praying for a long time
that God would raise up somebody in our ministry to
begin working with athletes."

Only a man like Bill Bright could fully appreciate
the vigor with which Hannah held his desire. Few men
alive today, perhaps none, possess the depth of
Bright's vision for reaching people for Christ. He was
the man God chose to believe Him for Arrowhead
Springs (Campus Crusade's international headquarters)
when there was no money for a down payment, and for
an evangelistic campaign to reach an incredible one
billion people for Christ.

Hannah had no intention of leaving Campus Crusade staff; he and Elaine planned to use the Rams'
salary to finance the new sports ministry.

After he arrived in Ram camp, Hannah's confidence became all the greater. The Rams were
desperate for a good kicker and Hannah looked like
their man. He won every kicking contest in camp.

However, the nagging discomfort Dave had experienced in his thighs before camp, now became acute
pain and stung sharply every time he moved. "I went
to Coach Allen about it," says Dave, "and he arranged
for me to have ultra-sound treatments.

"I kept kicking but before long I was in agony,"
Hannah continues. "They started giving me cortisone

shots. I would go to practice early just to get stretched out enough so I could move my legs; I couldn't run at all. I remember walking around outside at night and praying, "God, why don't you heal this thing?" I *knew* it was God's will for me to play pro football."

But the pain continued to worsen.

When players were cut from the Rams it was always done the same way. An assistant coach would inform maybe three or four players during breakfast that Coach Allen wanted to see them. Everybody knew what it meant. The players were seldom seen again.

One morning at breakfast Hannah was buttering his toast when he felt a tap on his shoulder. It was the assistant coach. "Coach Allen wants to see you right after you eat."

Dave stopped a moment, the toast sticking in his throat, looked over his shoulder to acknowledge the coach, and quietly finished his last meal as a Ram.

He found Allen in his office. The head coach minced no words. "We're going to have to let you go. There's no way you can play under game conditions."

Shortly after his release, Hannah quickly learned that former athletes no longer enjoy the same opportunities active athletes do. Active athletes are besieged by requests for speaking engagements; former athletes often find themselves besieged only by requests to get active athletes to speak. No one better understands the fleetingness of fame than a retired athlete—like Dave Hannah.

"A couple of nights after my release," he recalls, "I got a call from a guy wanting to know if I knew an athlete who could speak. They used to fly *me* different places to speak! But he wasn't interested in me now. I'd been cut . . . I became a nobody in the athletic world overnight."

Through the incident, Hannah, for the first time,

fully realized the significant opportunities that belong only to athletes—from the high schools to the colleges to the pros. Athletes are leaders and people listen to them. Hannah now resolved all the more to help Christian athletes take full advantage of the natural platform they command.

"Athletes," he reasons, "are used to sell everything from candy bars to cars. Why not have them tell about something far greater—the message of Jesus Christ?"

The Campus Crusade National Leadership Office at Arrowhead Springs was in touch with Hannah soon after his release.

"Dave, we've got an exciting challenge for you. Come up to Arrowhead and we'll talk to you about it."

"Exciting challenge!" Dave thought to himself. "I've got an exciting challenge right here. Just because I'm not with the Rams doesn't mean I can't start an athletic ministry." Hannah feared that Arrowhead had a different assignment in mind for him, and his fears were confirmed upon arriving at headquarters.

John Flack, the U.S. Field Director, chaired the Arrowhead meeting.

"Dave, our campus ministry at Michigan State needs someone like you to direct it. We want you to go up there and take over."

Dave cringed at the thought and replied bluntly, "I don't want to go to Michigan State. I want to start a ministry to athletes."

Flack spoke again, firmer, looking him in the eye. "I don't think you're man enough to do it."

The words pierced Hannah. He might have become angry had he not realized that what Flack said had a lot of validity.

"John, you're right. I'm not man enough to do it. Unless God is in it, it won't be successful."

Flack and his associates remained firm. They were

confident their decision best met the needs of Campus Crusade.

By the time he had finished the hour drive to Huntington Beach that day, Hannah was fuming. "If that's the way they're going to treat me I'll just leave staff." Disappointed and angry, he began to feel sorry for himself.

Hannah agonized for a week over the decision he had to make. "Should I leave staff? Where else am I going to start an athletic ministry? Michigan State isn't such a bad place," he thought. "But Dr. Bright was excited about my idea! Why this?"

It was a conversation with another staff member that eventually changed Dave's mode of thinking. Pat Matriciana had been a member of Dave's campus team at the University of Oklahoma.

"I thought you were willing to go wherever God wanted you," Matriciana probed one afternoon.

"I said I'm willing to go wherever *God* wants me, not where men want me."

"You're forgetting something, Dave. God works through men. He's in control of all things and *He* put them in authority over you."

Matriciana's words made Hannah realize something.

"I was essentially questioning God's sovereignty. This caused me to change the entire course of what I was saying and to rethink some things," Hannah said. "A few days later I was actually able to say, "All right, I'm willing to go to Michigan State. I don't want to go, it's not what I want, but if that's where you want me Lord, I'm willing to go."

And then came one of the biggest surprises in his 25 years. Amazingly it was John Flack who spoke the words.

"There's been a change of plans, Dave. We want

you to start an athletic ministry for Campus Crusade for Christ."

Hannah was thrilled but in his excitement did not forget the lesson he had learned. He realized he had been like the young boy who dropped his marble in a vase and got his hand trapped while trying to retrieve it. His parents worked and worked to free his trapped hand. The vase was a precious antique and his mother and father feared they must break it to free him. As they prepared to do so, the little boy asked, "Should I let go of the marble now?" He did, and found that with his fist unclenched, he was able to withdraw his hand easily from the vase.

"I was holding on to my dream of an athletic ministry tighter than the boy was holding on to that marble," Hannah says. "But God wanted me to let go. That was the only way I would learn it was *His* dream and *He* was going to do it, not me."

With the confirmed go-ahead from Campus Crusade, and now from the Lord, Hannah threw himself into his commission with typical Hannah zeal.

The "worldwide organization" that Hannah envisioned consisted then of a staff of two, Dave and Elaine. Their "headquarters" was a two-bedroom apartment in Tustin, a city located in the heart of southern California's Orange County.

With plenty of time on his hands, Dave spent hours drawing up organization charts, logos, crests and, of course, names for his ministry. "Athletes for Christ" was one possibility mentioned. Hannah the dreamer preferred "World Athletes for Christ."

A decision was eventually reached.

"The world name," Hannah explains, "was to be 'World Coaches and Athletes in Action' and the American name would be 'American Coaches and Athletes in Action.' Then we'd have an office in each country. The idea was that there would be a few of us running the world program and that each country would have their own program, their own colors and so on."

Hannah spared himself no delight when his perpetual dream machine was in gear. "I even had World Athletes in Action patches made up. The colors were white, green and gold. I had gold pants and a green sport coat with this crest on it. Then I had an American Athletes in Action outfit which was blue, gold and white, and of course, the American AIA crest and patch."

Hannah had to explain himself more than once. "I thought it was classic one day in front of a drive-in restaurant—I was the only guy in the world who had that crest on his coat and this girl says to me, 'What's World Athletes in Action?' I looked at her with an incredulous look on my face and said, 'You mean you don't know?' "

Dave's grandiose plans were not always a joking matter, at least not to Elaine, and especially not in the infant days of World Coaches and Athletes in Action. Such was the case the day the Hannahs sponsored a get-together for their financial support team in the back yard of Elaine's parent's home in Huntington Beach, California.

"Dave stood up and started telling about this athletic vision God had given him. I was mortified! I thought, 'It's one thing to tell my parents, but to tell our supporters is another thing! They'll think we're crazy!' "

Another early AIA project was the *Athletes in Action* magazine. "Dave, why on earth do you want a magazine?" people asked in consternation. Others had a sarcastic laugh at Hannah's expense . . . "Plan to feature a report from each of your continental offices, Dave?"

None of this daunted Hannah who began to write and recruit others to write for the first "World Coaches and Athletes in Action magazine."

Dave and Elaine were at Arrowhead Springs for some meetings when Dave pulled together the last of the material. He approached Elaine one day outside the Arrowhead hotel weighted down with rolls of interview tapes, dozens of note sheets, and reams of haphazardly stacked papers.

The fact that Dave was an aeronautical engineering major and not a journalism major was about to become painfully obvious.

"Well, here's our magazine, Elaine."

"Uh," stammered Elaine, "don't you think maybe it's a little long?"

"Oh, it's fine," Dave replied. "They'll take care of it."

"Well, don't you think somebody had better edit it?"

"Oh, they'll probably do that at the printers," Dave said.

"Dave, I don't think so. Why don't I read it?"

The publication deadline was near and Elaine labored to bring that magazine to life, sometimes toiling 18 hours a day while Dave was out of town. She had no journalistic experience but proved a quick learner—the hard way.

Elaine picked Dave up a few days later after his trip and the tired couple stopped for dinner before heading to the Arrowhead hotel for the night.

"I've finished rewriting and typing the stories," Elaine said. "Why don't I bring them inside so we can take a look over dinner?"

"Oh, I'm tired of that," Dave said. "Let's talk about something else." Elaine was even more tired of it and readily agreed.

It wasn't until the next morning that the couple realized someone had broken into their car during dinner and stolen the entire draft of the magazine.

"We would have been totally lost," Elaine said, "because I had thrown away all the extra and scratch copies of the stories. But one night, for no reason, I woke up and went outside to the trash can and pulled out all the rough copy. Now I know why."

The Hannahs stayed at Arrowhead for three days and worked almost around the clock to redo the magazine. They didn't change clothes once during the three days; they couldn't—whoever snatched the magazine copy had stolen their suitcases as well!

One of the first staff members assigned to Hannah was Larry Tregoning. Tregoning had captained the number two nationally-ranked basketball team for Michigan, the year before. Hannah needed the athlete for a revolutionary project that required very special skills.

The idea for the project came to Hannah one day as he watched a Campus Crusade music group share an evangelistic message through its performance. Hannah thought out loud, "Why couldn't an athletic team be used in the same way? Yeah! Why not?" The dream-machine wheels shifted into high gear, setting in motion what is now the Athletes in Action USA basketball team.

One person Hannah shared his idea with was UCLA Basketball Coach John Wooden. Wooden liked the idea, but didn't think the big schools would schedule the Christian team.

Hannah and Tregoning journeyed to the NCAA Coaches Convention in Louisville, Kentucky, and approached a number of coaches to talk about their team.

"I didn't know who a lot of them were," Hannah said, "so I walked around looking at their name tags. When I saw a coach of a major university I approached him and said, 'Hi, I'm Dave Hannah with Athletes in Action'."

Hannah then quickly introduced Tregoning. Instantly recognizable, the former Michigan star lent credibility. Together they explained the revolutionary concept of a team that would play basketball against the top colleges in the nation and use the halftime break to tell its audience how they can know Christ personally.

The coach of one West Coast university proved an especially "spirited" helper. "This guy drank all the time at the convention," Hannah recalls, "and he's the kind of guy who gets real 'happy' when he gets drunk.

"He took us around to all his friends, and with his arm around me, he'd say, 'Hey, you've got to play these guys. These guys are really good!'

"But when he sobered up," Hannah added, "he didn't want to play us. He did stick to his commitment that first year, though."

Amazingly, not a single coach asked who was on the new team. It might have been embarrassing—Tregoning was the only player!

Hannah and Tregoning, with a giant step of faith, had come up with a 27-game schedule. But now loomed the larger question—could they come up with a basketball team?

CHAPTER THREE

GROWING PAINS

*"Let's face it—you guys are cannon fodder for
the good teams."*

A Sportswriter

It was going to take quality players, that much was
for sure. But recruiting quality players to a team that
doesn't exist is an outlandish, if not impossible, under-
taking. Imagine recruiting a high school all-American to
a college that hasn't been founded!

One of the players the recruiters called was Bill
Bradley, the great all-American from Princeton. The
fact that Bradley was in England studying on a Rhodes
scholarship didn't dissuade them.

"Hello, Bill, this is Larry Tregoning from Michigan.
I held you to 44 points. Remember me?"

Bradley remembered, but he was unimpressed by
Tregoning's offer as well as his defense.

The AIA recruiting program consisted mostly of
prayer. What else is a recruiter to do whose "pitch"
sounds like this . . . On the schedule: "We play some of
the best teams in the country but probably won't beat
many of them." On salary: "We don't pay much and
you have to raise your own money."

Support raising, or "deputation," as it is called in
missionary circles, requires that each member finance
his personal involvement in the ministry by contacting
interested churches and individuals to obtain monthly

commitments. The practice was enough to convince more than one basketball player he was called elsewhere: "Raise my own *what*?"

One player who agreed to come with the team, former Wisconsin leading scorer Ken Gustafson, changed his mind about support raising.

"I'm quitting," he said by phone from his hometown, "I can't raise my support."

"Oh yes you can!" Hannah quickly assured him. "You've got to!" Gustafson eventually made it.

The practice of support raising proved a blessing to those who were indeed called. It provided a "faith-stretching" time for players as they saw God fulfill His promises--"And my God shall supply all your needs according to His riches in glory in Christ Jesus" (Philippians 4:19).

Players had to be athletically *and* spiritually qualified for this unique team. Tregoning was not opposed, however, to the idea of mixing recruiting and evangelism. He led one basketball player to Christ after meeting him during a pick-up game in a San Bernardino, California city park. He and Hannah began meeting with the new believer to help him grow in his faith. DeWayne Brewer, a 6-foot-3 guard, eventually joined the AIA team.

"The players are coming, but where are we going to find a coach?" Hannah asked Tregoning late one night in a cramped Arrowhead hotel office.

"I don't know," Tregoning muttered. "Keep praying."

The head basketball coach at the University of Alaska, a young Christian, had recently resigned his position. Campus Crusade staff member Fred Dyson was quickly in touch by phone urging him to come to Arrowhead Springs "for just three weeks" to help start a "Christian basketball team."

The coach, Fred Crowell, figured that Dyson wanted

more than a mere three-week commitment—he wanted a full-time coach. "Nothing repulsed me more than the idea of becoming a missionary," Crowell admits.

He wrote the staff member a long letter filled with apologies, especially the fact that he had already made a commitment to a doctoral fellowship. Crowell sent the letter air mail, special delivery—"I thought this would get him off my back politely."

But several days later Dyson called again. "The team is in desperate straits," he said. "There's no organization or supervision. Won't you just come for three weeks?"

Crowell was puzzled. "Dyson sounded like he didn't get my letter." For some reason Crowell and his wife, Susie, felt compelled to go to California. The coach gave in. "But don't feel hurt," he warned Dyson, "when I climb on a plane in three weeks and leave again."

Immediately upon arrival at Arrowhead Springs, Crowell learned that Dyson had not received his letter. In fact, he didn't receive it until a month later. Had Dyson received the message when he should have, he never would have called.

"As the days passed," Crowell recalls, "I was in tremendous turmoil." The couple was beginning to feel led to stay on with the basketball team full-time, and Fred, for one, didn't like it. Even the obstacle of their contractual obligations was removed: Fred was released from his doctoral agreement, and the assistant superintendent of a public school district released Susie from her contract on the "last possible day."

Crowell was out of excuses. And in three short weeks God had changed his heart dramatically. "I guess this is where God wants me," he said. The Athletes in Action basketball team had its coach.

After drilling for what one player said "seemed like an eternity," the team was ready for some preliminary games against small colleges and AAU teams. The "Chargers," as Hannah dubbed the squad, won all six of these contests. But California Baptist and "Manny's Coasters" are a far cry from major college competition.

"Can we do it against *real* competition?" the players wondered. They also wondered how their evangelistic message, presented during halftime and after games, would be received by a university audience that expected to see basketball *only.* "Nobody threw stones at us during the preliminary games," Cliff Cox said, "so we figured it would be all right."

After dropping its first major game to the University of Utah, the team got some bad news. Crowell's scouting report labeled Utah a good team but Wichita State, the second opponent, a great team.

"I could see Wichita beating us by 100 points," said Hannah, who went along on the team's first trip. "We had to get up at four in the morning for our flight to Denver after the Utah game. After being delayed in the Denver airport for five hours, the plane finally took off only to land in a snowstorm in Wichita. People were supposed to meet us there, but nobody showed up."

The weary team rented cars and stopped only for a quick dinner before hurrying to the 11,000-seat Henry Levitt Arena for the game. "Two minutes before the game started, there were maybe a thousand people there," Hannah recalls. "Five minutes later the place was full . . . and they were *loud.*"

American Athletes in Action quickly fell to the short end of a 23-5 score. "Time-out!" Fred Crowell yelled. The 25-year-old coach had always dreamed of coaching in big-time basketball but admits, "My dream certainly had not included being slaughtered!"

The time-out had its intended effect. The team, more settled, took charge and not only made up the 18-

point deficit but actually led at halftime by two. As forward Ricky Mill was telling the audience about his personal relationship with Christ during intermission, a radio broadcast announcer overheard him and exclaimed to his audience: "Wait a minute. These guys are talking about Christ! You have to hear what they are saying." He then took his microphone out to the floor to pick up the team's presentation.

The Campus Crusade team let the game slip away in the final minutes, falling 97-89, but had proved it was capable of playing with the big universities. More importantly, over 300 people indicated decisions for Christ. Such was the story of the first season—more than 75,000 people in live audiences heard the claims of Christ and hundreds of lives were changed.

The team also managed a 15-14 winning record. A winning slate in *any* team's inaugural season is a noteworthy accomplishment (ask the 1980-81 Dallas Mavericks who finished 15-67).

"We're on our way now," Hannah sensed. "This is just the beginning."

Hannah was wrong. Despite a good recruiting year, the team slipped to 14-17 for the second year. The next two campaigns were no better: 22-24 and 13-16.

Hannah and Crowell agonized over how to turn the team's fortunes around. One night after an especially tough loss they sat up until 3 in the morning, playing "table-top football," while analyzing every aspect of the team.

Both men grasped what winning could do for a program like World Coaches and Athletes in Action. Hannah believed it would revolutionize Campus Crusade's young athletic ministry. His argument was convincing: "Who has the better attendance—first-place or last-place teams? Who is featured in the newspapers more—the nations's finest or the also-rans? Who do people write about, talk about, pay to see? Winners!'"

It was a simple matter in Hannah's mind. "The better we are, the more people will watch us. The more people who watch us, the more we reach for Christ."

But it was the media possibilities that excited, and frustrated, Hannah most. Millions could potentially be exposed to the claims of Christ via interviews and features with AIA athletes and teams in the secular media. That was exciting. But it wasn't happening. That was frustrating.

The basketball team *did* receive press coverage, and it was positive. It was also limited. The stories that appeared were of a predictable variety, pointing out what "sacrifices these young men are making." News stories just told who won or lost. For some reason, reporters weren't curious enough to write about the *purpose* of the team. Sometimes a visit to a city was barely acknowledged by the media.

Fred Crowell resigned in the spring of 1971, citing a desire to spend more time with his wife and his daughter who was ill. Greg Berry took over in 1971-72.

That season the team sank even lower, finishing 7-21, but the factors that kept the team from winning were no mystery. The problems, though easily identifiable, were not easily solved.

There were, however, positive aspects to even the most severe problems. The money shortage, for example, caused the men to be the best stewards of the money they did have. One of the ways the team economized was by staying in private homes instead of hotels. That practice provided many opportunities for ministry and fellowship, but didn't make winning any easier. Hosts sometimes seemed determined that their guests be entertained *and* unable to play basketball.

Consider:—Dennis Cantrell, a player between 1970-73, and his wife Lyn, who was with him on the team's annual wives trip, stayed with a woman who "entertained" on her piano until 2 a.m. At 6 a.m., after the bedraggled couple had finally fallen asleep, she burst into their room unannounced with a grapefruit tray, crooning "Oh What a Beautiful Morning."

—A pastor's wife in Wichita, Kansas, spent hours preparing a lavish meal for her guest, Bill Hull. Hull, already nicknamed "The Load" because of a weight problem, tried to explain kindly that he could not eat potatoes and chicken and dumplings—especially not two hours before a game! The pastor's wife, greatly insulted, said she would never again allow another basketball player in her home.

—Arrangements to house the players were quickly made during a trip to Alaska when blizzard conditions in Anchorage made a planned postgame trip to a neighboring city impossible. "We'll put a couple of the fellas up," one man volunteered. Cantrell and Larry Gatewood went with the man to his house, a dilapidated trailer. There they were shown to a cramped bedroom. The players were stunned enough that they would be sleeping together on a tiny metal frame bed that dominated the dinky room. But they incredulously stared at a gaping hole in the trailer wall, through which an icy arctic wind was howling. "We just looked at each other, slowly shook our heads and climbed in," Dennis said.

—Still another hostess was "crazy" about her guests. The woman stayed up all night, pacing back and forth outside the guest bedroom. "I couldn't hear her but I could see her shadow passing every 30 seconds," Jimmy Walker remembers. "Jim (another player) told me to go to sleep, but no way; I was afraid of what she might do!"

As limited as the team budget was, the players operated under even tighter personal constraints. Bill Hull, a player between 1969-71 and again in 1972-73, remembers getting help from a teammate when his funds ran low. "I shook hands with Cliff Cox one day and found a $5.00 bill in my hand," Hull said. "In 1969 that was a third of a week's groceries." "Eggs again?" Dennis often groaned. "I never knew they could be cooked so many ways."

The team's recruiting problems were perpetuated by the fact that the squad continued to lose. Even a committed Christian is hesitant to join a loser, regardless of ministry opportunities. The recruiting deficiencies showed most in AIA's lack of good, big centers during the early years.

The fact that Hannah was busy overseeing other facets of the rapidly-expanding AIA ministry limited the time he could devote to the basketball team's development.

Wrestling, track and field, weightlifting and gymnastic teams had been formed and others were on the drawing boards. Pat Matriciana and John Klein, a capable new staff member from Minnesota, organized the wrestling team which had a 52-10-1 record under head coach Gene Davis after four seasons. Perhaps even more significant, the wrestlers had as much (or more) success getting their message out through the secular media as did the basketball team despite the fact that basketball is a far more popular sport in the United States.

The ministry *could* have expanded even more. A steady flow of people approached Hannah with ideas — some good, some not so good, the variety of which staggered even *his* imagination. One aspirant wanted to start an AIA water ski team: "After the show, we'll pull the boat up near shore and proclaim the gospel. Isn't that what Jesus did?"

Craig Harriman wanted to start a rodeo team. His bucking broncos never got off the drawing board and into the corral, but Harriman later found his niche as an administrator with AIA.

"Dave would talk to somebody who had some new idea," says Klein, now an assistant national director. "He'd come back all excited and we'd have to talk him out of it."

Weightlifter Russ Knipp joined AIA in the fall of 1969 and became its first Olympic competitor. He and Hannah were a part of a touring AIA weightlifting team that spoke to more than 500,000 people in four years. It was also near this time that Dr. Bright suggested that the "World Coaches" and "American" prefixes to Athletes in Action be dropped, shortening the name to simply "Athletes in Action."

In the fall of 1972 AIA split its basketball team into two squads: the existing team would become "AIA East" and be based in Indianapolis, Indiana; "AIA West" was formed and based in Phoenix, Arizona. The reorganization succeeded in enlarging total audience size and in cutting travel costs, but worsened another problem — Hannah now had *two* mediocre basketball teams.

By 1974, Athletes in Action staff, now numbering over 150, were located in a number of headquarters around the country:

> East Wrestling — Lancaster, Pa.
> West Wrestling — Long Beach, Calif.
> Weightlifting — Tulsa, Okla.
> Track — Santa Ana, Calif.
> Tennis — Garland, Texas
> Gymnastics — La Mesa, Calif.

The national expansion meant increased travel for Dave. Elaine was finally able to accept Dave's being away, but it hadn't always been that way. His absences once caused fear bordering on paranoia in Elaine. She was terrified and continually burst into tears — sometimes weeks before he left!

"It was the same way when my father was out of town during my childhood," Elaine says. "I was afraid to be alone. When Dave left town I actually piled furniture in front of the door. Then I was up most of the night, pacing back and forth, peeking out the windows."

One day while the couple was still serving in the campus ministry, Elaine drove Dave to the Oklahoma City airport for a typically emotional send-off. "Don't go," she pleaded.

Bear in mind that this emotional scene took place in the late 60s when the Vietnam War had reached its peak and many wives knew it would be months before they saw their departing husbands again, if ever.

An older woman noticed Elaine, arms wrapped around her husband, crying hysterically. "You poor dear," she said compassionately. "Where is your husband being sent?"

He's going . . ." Elaine stammered between sobs, ". . . to Tulsa . . . for the night."

The young wife was beginning to think she and Dave should not be on Campus Crusade staff: "What's the use of being married if your husband is gallivanting around the world all the time?

"I resented Campus Crusade and this whole athletic ministry for taking Dave away from me," Elaine said. "Then one day I decided I should do something about it."

The problem had come to a head during one of Dave's longer trips. "I knew I was in for a bad time as soon as he left," Elaine remembers. "We had just moved into a new house, and it didn't take long for me to realize that there were more doors than there was furniture."

After three sleepless nights, Elaine was a physical

and emotional wreck. "I'm not going to last until he gets home, I thought." Until now, she had prayed that God would change either the situation or Dave's mind. Now she prayed that God would change her attitude. "I fell into bed exhausted and the next thing I knew it was seven o'clock and the sun was shining." The fear was gone. It never returned.

"I'm glad the Lord taught me what He did before I manipulated Dave out of God's will," Elaine says.

For his part, Dave recognized that he must guard his priorities. "My walk with God and my family must come before work," he says, "be that 'ministry work' or not. It's my responsibility before God to keep my priorities straight." For Dave, that includes spending quality time alone with Elaine and their two sons, Eric and Scott, born in 1967 and 1970, respectively.

"If Christ is on the throne of my life where *He* belongs, everything else seems to fall into place," Hannah says.

Like Hannah, the early AIA basketball players understood that Christ must be first. This was evident in their ministry. The fruit of their hard work was not always evident on the basketball court. But their diligence was evident in lives that were touched.

On one occasion in Toledo, Ohio, the team spoke at 17 different high school assemblies. During the last assembly, so tired was Fred Crowell that he fell asleep in one of the team cars outside the school, and had to be awakened to drive to the game that night.

Another team visited Birmingham, Alabama, and performed an incredible 200 speaking engagements in just one week.

A high school assembly in Boise, Idaho, stands out most in Cliff Cox's mind. "They wouldn't let us close our presentation in prayer," Cox said, "so we closed it by saying, 'If you want to know how you can come to know Christ personally, be sure to come to the game tomorrow night at Boise State.' "

"Afterward, as I was walking out through the parking lot, I'll never forget the young guy who hurried out to me. 'Mister,' he said, 'I can't come to the game tomorrow night. Can you tell me right now how I can know Christ?' "

Cox and the high school student stood together in the parking lot and prayed and the student asked Christ to be his Savior.

In 1969 the team had an exciting ministry during a 20-game, 26-day tour of South America. In Chile, several of the players were introduced to a very attractive woman. The woman said she could no longer listen, night after night, to them talk about the love, peace and joy they were experiencing. The team had played in three different cities in Chile, each many miles from the others, so the players were amazed she had seen all three games. They asked how this was possible.

"I am too ashamed to tell you," was her response. Then reluctantly, with tears flowing, she told how she was the mistress of a Chilean official who was traveling with the AIA team. She realized that she needed to break off the relationship. The players joined in prayer for her and rejoiced when she did break off the relationship and when she experienced God's forgiveness.

The team once visited Camp Pendleton near San Diego, California, and gave an evangelistic message. The audience, 2,000 Marines, was much larger than expected and remarkably attentive. "They hung onto every word," said Clint Hooper, a star player on the team. "They were intense."

Talking to the Camp Pendleton chaplain later, the

players found out why. "Many of these guys will never see America again," he said. "They're going to Vietnam in a few days."

Meanwhile, the ministry, flourishing on a small scale, still needed an athletic boost to multiply its impact.

It looked like the West team, at least, would get that help when Jim King signed on as head coach in 1973. King, a former NBA player and coach (Chicago Bulls) brought increased credibility to the AIA program. Plans to televise some of the team's games were put into motion. The development of the West team was to be emphasized.

King's signing was indeed a breakthrough. The coach led the West team to a combined 55-24 record in his two years at the helm (the East team continued to struggle at a sub-.500 pace). King's impact, however, was not the panacea Hannah had hoped for. The majority of the team's wins came against small colleges and AAU teams. Only a handful came at the expense of major universities; in fact, few major schools were even scheduled. And the media response, on a national basis, was virtually nil.

An effort was made to generate interest with the media. *Sports Illustrated* was one of many periodicals contacted. "We're interested in covering top quality sports," a man at the magazine's Los Angeles office responded. "If you fit into that category, fine. But let's face it — you guys are cannon fodder for the good teams."

The man had a point. Though the West team's cumulative record, in 1974-75 was 30-13, the squad was just 10-11 against colleges. After eight basketball seasons it seemed that very little had changed. The program was stuck on a treadmill . . . and there was little reason to believe it would soon get off.

The television project had been postponed, then cancelled. Jim King resigned to coach at Tulsa University. Nearly two-thirds of the West team called it quits at about the same time.

This was a discouraging time for Hannah. It was also a time that drew him closer to Elaine. He knew he needed her. She was his sounding board and a comfort to him. "God can use the team whether they win or lose," Elaine said. "You know that."

"That's true," Dave agreed. "But this ministry is only a fraction of what it could be. Imagine the impact we could have through the sports media. If we had a basketball team good enough to put on TV we could reach more people in one night than we have reached in the last eight years."

But for now, Hannah was out of ideas. "Elaine, I just don't know what else to try."

The newness of the team's unique purpose had long since worn off. It was becoming apparent that if AIA did not develop, it might even have trouble scheduling the better amateur teams in the country.

"Maybe," Dave thought out loud, "maybe I'm just not the one that God wants to use to take this program where it needs to go."

Dave Hannah was ready to do something he had never done before . . . quit.

CHAPTER
FOUR

A HEART FOR GOD GROWS ON THE FARM

*"Life is so temporary; it can end any time. I
don't want to look back on my life some day
and see waste . . . I want fruit that will remain."*

Dave Hannah

When David Robert Hannah was a young boy
growing up in tiny Alden, Iowa, he didn't want to go to
heaven. People in heaven,"were angels who floated
around on the clouds, playing harps and singing
music." He couldn't play, couldn't sing — he couldn't
even sit still — so he figured, "What's there in heaven
for me?"

He thought that if you couldn't be anything else,
you became a Christian. In young Dave's mind, if you
were a man's man, you couldn't be a Christian.

He seldom attended church. When he did it was
the little Methodist church about a half-mile from the
Hannah farm on Route 2 just outside of Alden. The
Hannahs were regular church attenders —-every
Christmas and Easter.

"That was over-exposure as far as I was concerned," Dave admits.

He was even less likely to attend any of the
Methodist Youth Fellowship (MYF) activities. But one
Sunday night, a teenage buddy talked him into going

47

to one of the meetings. Some of the neighbor kids had been looking for a way to get him involved in the group. One guy thought he had the answer. This particular night happened to be the group's annual election.

"I nominate Dave Hannah for president," he said.

Caught by surprise, David R. didn't know quite how to react. So he did nothing. And since no one else from the group of 10 was nominated, the unsuspecting visitor won a smashing, unanimous victory. Hannah reveled in the congratulatory atmosphere ("What else *can* I do!" he thought.)

A week later the same MYF'ers gathered again, but to their consternation the new leader didn't show up. He never showed up again! Dave Hannah wasn't ready to get involved in *any* church, and it would be a while yet before he was ready to take his first — and last — stab at elected office.

Hannah's abhorrence for church involvement, seems paradoxical since he was always interested in the things of God. Often during the years just pre- ceding his teens he would inform his parents and maternal grandfather who lived with the family — "I'm holding church!" Mom, Dad and Grandpa would dutifully file into the living room where Dave would lead them in some hymns and prayer, then deliver a message which consisted of whatever was on his mind about God at the time.

One factor that may have kept him away from the institution was a fear of large groups. Dave Hannah was, and still is in many ways, a loner. Not so much by choice, but by the demands of his environment as a child. He grew up as an "only child" on a farm outside of town. Removed from extended contacts with people, he was a slow developer socially. To this day he doesn't meet people well, and often comes across as cold at first meeting despite his inner warmth.

Even had the Hannahs lived in town it would not have been a cultural paradise. Alden, Iowa — located between Dows and Popejoy — is not one of America's livelier, more cosmopolitan cities. In fact, calling Alden a city at all is stretching things. A community of some 200 farmers and their families with assorted "city" workers is more like it.

As an only child, Dave learned to entertain himself. He was one of the few people in the world who could play football by himself. Grabbing the ball off the ground, he would run twisting and turning through the backyard until an invisible tackler knocked him down. The aspiring athlete often pretended that two Big Ten Conference schools were battling and his natural prejudice for the local Iowa teams sometimes showed. In one edition of Hannah's "football solitaire" the University of Iowa beat Ohio State 70-3!

The youngster didn't get away with playing games all day, of course. One of Dave's many duties was to pitch silage, a pungent mass of rotten corn used to feed animals, each morning before he went to school. Consequently, there was no mistaking Dave Hannah when he entered the schoolroom. The residue odor gave him away and earned him a hated nickname — "silage foot!"

Many of the youngster's chores involved helping with the family restaurant business. Actually, the Hannahs never planned to be in the restaurant business — it just sort of evolved. Bill and Dorothy Hannah, Dave's parents, often entertained friends and soon the practice became so common (and the food so good) that friends started coming more and offering to pay.

It didn't take long for Bill Hannah, a true entrepreneur, to recognize the profit potential and

"Hannah's Guest Farm," as it came to be called, was soon serving up nightly rounds of the house specialty — steaks, all from aged beef, hickory-smoked pork chops, baked potatoes, garlic bread with a cheese topping, house salad dressings and homemade ice cream.

The Hannahs made their home available to out-of-town guests who wanted to stay overnight. The business grew until it was something akin to a smaller version of a modern dude ranch.

Each family member had a job to do. "I watched the kids," says Dave. "We generally had families from all over the country. When I got older, I started helping in the kitchen."

Bill Hannah was the owner, the boss, the chief cook and advertising director. His favorite advertising innovation was a wooden sign tacked to a tree. The tree stood next to the road which passed an earthen dam near their house. The sign read:

"HANNAH'S GUEST FARM
BEST FOOD BY A DAM SITE"

The nightly gatherings in Dave's living room did nothing to subdue the loneliness of ranch life for the teenager. While there were a lot of people around, they were mostly older and Dave continued to feel uncomfortable around groups.

He eventually moved his room into the basement where he salvaged what privacy he could. Hannah still covets his privacy, and probably always will. "I don't need a lot of social life," he says. "I'm happy just being home with my wife and family."

It was high school — more specifically high school athletics — that helped Dave begin to overcome his shyness. Lettering in four sports (football, baseball, basketball and track) and making all-state in the first three is no easy accomplishment.

Socially, he made strides during the high school years, but fell far short of the performance he mustered later in college. In fact, the girls used to joke about a typical date with Dave Hannah.

"I would take them to Hannah's Guest Farm for a nice steak dinner, then five miles over to Iowa Falls to see a picture show, then home. That's it. There was *never* any holding hands or kissing. Nobody ever told me how you were supposed to operate," he says. "After about five dates I got labeled. It never occurred to me to do anything different."

Upon entering Consolidated High School Dave got his first and last taste of elected office when he ran for freshman class president "because it seemed like the thing to do." He won the election handily, but his first project as class president — the homecoming float — turned out to be headache enough for him to swear off politics for life.

"I'm through with leading people. No more elected offices, no more leadership," he vowed. He kept the first part.

As a freshman Dave stood 5-feet-10; he was 6-feet-0 as a sophomore, and by the time his junior year arrived, he had grown to 6-feet-3 and packed 200 muscled pounds on his frame. Combine that with a 10.1 100-yard dash clocking and presto — you have the credentials of a bluechip college recruit.

But visits from college recruiters were few and far between to out-of-the-way Alden, especially when winter temperatures often plunged near 30-below.

Dave's lone contact was Ralph Higgins, the Oklahoma State track coach, a friend of the family and a frequent visitor at the Hannah house. With each visit during Dave's high school years he got an earful of accolades from the elder Hannah.

"Ralph, the kid's got potential,"Bill would say. "Why you should have seen him the other night against Colorado. Four touchdowns, 240 yards on the ground."

"That's great . . ." Ralph would get in before Bill continued.

"Now you and I both know I'm prejudiced — because he's my boy, right? So you oughta get one of those football scouts down here to check him out for yourself. You know he's up to 210 now . . . .

Bill Hannah, 275 pounds of natural-born salesman, left an indelible mark on his son's life. But Dad was not the only one who helped Dave along the way . . . or tried to.

The Alden High School principal, Fred Hilton, also interceded for Dave via a letter to Iowa State University that scolded the Cyclones for, among other things, giving scholarships to out-of-state athletes — not "*our* good athletes." Hilton, after remarking that he would be "interested to hear . . . the usual excuses" for the losing football team this fall, concluded his letter: "Thanks for everything and remember we are still looking forward to the day we can see a good team on the field at Iowa State University."

The principal's letter proved no help, but Oklahoma State scouted Dave twice as a senior, once in football and once in basketball. He had his best game ever on both occasions — including a 28-rebound basketball effort — unaware that a scout was sitting in the stands. OSU offered him scholarships in both sports the following spring. He accepted the football offer.

It was in college that the farm boy's social growth finally began to match his earlier physical growth. And it was again his father who gave him the push he needed, though it wasn't intended that way.

Bill Hannah had another of his "chance" meetings, this time with Otis Wile, the sports editor of the *Stillwater News-Press*. Afterward, Wile wrote a piece that began: "Talked at some length with a personable fellow named William D. Hannah of Alden, Ia. . . ." The sports editor concluded his story with a winsome comment on Hannah's blue-chip boy: "We would wager a bob or two that he'll fit in somewhere and make himself a happy home here on the range."

If nothing else, the article served to make Dave the most sought-after freshman when it came time for fraternity rush.

The rush pitches haven't changed a lot in the last 20 years, and they sounded "oh so attractive" to a farm boy who since junior high school had attended school with the same 12 girls.

"Dave, come on over to the house tonight. There's a party and some of the little sisters want to meet you."

He eventually decided on Beta Theta Pi, which most agreed was the top fraternity on campus.

The thrill of being a campus big-shot didn't last long. It only took a few trips to the football practice field to humble Hannah and every other aspiring freshman.

Hannah tore ligaments in his knee during that first season and didn't see any game action. Injuries limited his football achievements throughout his four-year career with the Cowboys. In addition to the torn knee, he suffered two separated shoulders and a drawn-out bout with mononucleosis.

It was in his special task as a punter that Hannah enjoyed real success. Once, against Wichita State, he had a punt travel the length of the field and roll all the way out of the opposite end zone.

The college years were good ones for Hannah: the fact that he was on the football team gave him status on campus, his studies were going well as he worked toward a degree in engineering, and his social life was never better. That had barely existed at all before, and anything would have been an improvement, but at OSU he made up for time lost on the farm. In one year alone he spent $2,000 on dates!

But, strangely the status and the social life — these things he had always wanted — didn't satisfy him.

"I began thinking to myself, 'If this is the good life, then why am I not contented? I play football, I'm well-known, I'm going to make money when I graduate . . . so what! I don't have a purpose in life.' "

Hannah's honest self-examination readied him to hear about a new way of life when the opportunity came.

Dave first heard the message that would change his life when he met Swede Anderson, the University of Colorado's student body president (and now director of Campus Crusade's Christian Embassy ministry). Anderson asked Dave to lunch, and it was in a restaurant that Dave Hannah bowed his head and trusted Christ as Savior.

The new convert did not grow in his faith over-night, but after a Campus Crusade staff member named Robert Andrews began to teach him from the Bible, he embraced his new faith with a passion.

The 21-year-old student decided that he was going to evangelize the OSU campus, and maybe the world when he could get to it. He was soon taking part in revival meetings, speaking in churches all over the state of Oklahoma. Practicing for hours to perfect a booming, old-time preacher's voice, he climbed into the pulpit and thundered out against Communism, sin and the evils of money.

On one occasion the pastor of the church asked his congregation, "Now who's going to invite this young preacher home for a meal?" Nobody would do it! The pastor ended up with the young fire-breather in *his* home.

It didn't take long for the new believer's natural leadership ability to emerge and soon he was one of the key students in the Oklahoma State Campus Crusade movement.

By the time he went home the following summer he was a new person. Gone was the temper that had often flared up. Gone was the lack of direction and purpose that had beset him. He had a new joy about him, new attitudes — and his parents couldn't help but notice.

"Dave, there's something different about you," his mother said to him as she prepared to put dinner on the table one night.

"Yes, there really is, Mom, and I want to tell you and Dad about it sometime," Dave replied.

Fortunately, it didn't take him long to get around to it. His parents were ready to receive Christ; in fact, both of them were probably ready years before but had never understood how. They prayed to receive Christ.

Both parents began to grow in their faith, too, especially Dave's mother. Bill and Dorothy began regularly attending the little Methodist church they had neglected so long. As it happened, Dorothy Hannah was much closer to her appointed time to enter God's kingdom than anyone realized.

Having returned to school for his senior year in the fall, Dave was back in the mill of his activities, when, one morning at 4 a.m., the call came at the Beta house. The Hannah's next door neighbor bore the news.

"Dave, your mother has died," he said softly.

Something inside Dave wrenched at the words.

Dorothy Hannah was preparing to go home after being in the hospital for cancer treatment. But on the day she was to have been released she suffered a heart attack and died. The fact that the death was not a total surprise did little to diminish the pain.

After he finished talking with his neighbor, Dave slumped down in the phone booth inside the fraternity house and prayed. This was the only place in the house where he could be alone. Strangely enough, he came there often for this very reason.

Later, walking outside, he thought to himself, "Life is so temporary; it can end any time. I don't want to look back on my life some day and see waste ... I want fruit that will remain," he resolved. "And only God's fruit remains."

This was the beginning of a philosophy, a new set of convictions. It's been called a "kingdom mentality." Simply, it means putting God first. The priority is God's will — seeking Him and matters of eternal consequence first — rather than pursuing the temporary rewards that this world offers.

Hannah's desire to have an impact for Christ became more intense. He decided to take part in a Campus Crusade "student staff" program that took him to UCLA where he could study under Hal Lindsey who was then the campus director. He figured he could take some classes at the same time and work toward his degree.

He had only been at UCLA a few weeks when he first laid eyes on Elaine. It was at Lindsey's house, at a meeting for student leaders. She was an attractive coed and he was impressed.

She was impressed, too, albeit to a lesser extent.

When Dave walked in, Elaine said to herself, "Hmm, I think I'll take him," meaning, "I'll see what I can do to get him to ask me out."

Looking back, Elaine knows that it had to be of the Lord. "Dave wasn't a whole lot to look at at the time," Elaine said. "He quit lifting weights after football and didn't have much money, so he could afford only one meal a day," she added.

"I shrank from 235 pounds down to 175 in a matter of a few months," Dave recalls.

The coed's confidence in her ability to interest the young man was not unwarranted. The 21-year-old was one of the most popular girls on the Westwood campus; on several occasions she had two dates in one day! It wasn't hard to get Dave to take notice. He asked her out within a matter of days.

The "no" reply he got set him back. "This never happened back at Oklahoma State," he thought.

"I've got another date," Elaine explained.

"Dogged Dave" didn't give up. He'd never been a quitter and this setback made him all the more determined. He once went so far as to ask Elaine for a date a month in advance. Elaine became a little worried at this point.

"Before, I'd always grown tired of guys after a month. And to be honest, I kept thinking that I would eventually dump him."

But Elaine was intrigued by this tall, skinny fellow from Iowa. She admired his persistence even though she "knew he was wasting his time."

Before long, though, Elaine "began coming around," according to Dave. The two started to look for creative ways to spend time together. "It seemed like every time Dave was to speak some place, the campus director would call me up and ask me to go along to give my testimony," Elaine said. "It didn't take long for me to figure out he was moonlighting as a matchmaker."

As the two spent more time together, Dave realized

"this is the girl for me!" and decided it was time to share his true feelings with her. He took her on a romantic drive one night up Mulholland Drive to his church, Bel Air Presbyterian, and they enjoyed an inspiring view of Los Angeles below.

"Elaine," Dave said, gazing into her eyes, "I want you to know that I love you."

"Uh, I like you, too," she said quickly. This was not exactly what the young troubadour had hoped to hear!

Later, the memory of those words came back to wake Dave up in the middle of the night. "I bolted upright in my bed and all I could hear was 'I like you, I like you' over and over in my mind! 'I like you'!"

Following that evening their time together was limited. Dave returned to Iowa for Christmas and then journeyed back to OSU for the spring term in which he took 22 academic units in a frantic attempt to finish school. He somehow found time for weightlifting among his studies and bulked himself back up — and over — what he had ever been to, 265 pounds! He returned to California for a visit in June before starting his last semester at Oklahoma State.

Elaine didn't recognize Dave at first sight. "Dave . . . is that you?" Elaine said in disbelief. "What happened!" she laughed, giving him a friendly hug.

It was the ensuing weeks together, with phone calls, other visits and letters between the visits, that finally won Elaine's heart. They were married in Orange County, California in February of 1965. Dave had earlier joined the staff of Campus Crusade for Christ, and now, together, the new husband and wife team watched the ministry Dave directed at the University of Oklahoma multiply. In two short years the movement blossomed from a core of just eight to more than 300 involved students.

Their relationship blossomed, too. That marriage was God's sovereign way of strengthening the two to face the trials that lay ahead.

And after eight years with Athletes in Action, the trials were just beginning for Hannah. Each year the director had to face dark moments of discouragement. At times, it was tempting to simply walk away from it all; 1975 was one of those times.

Now it was Elaine's turn to be strong. She asked Dave, "Can you think of any place where you can have a greater impact for Christ?"

Dave answered with silence. He knew this was the issue that mattered most. In the final analysis, Hannah could not seriously consider leaving. God had not *called* him away.

"God has done some great things in the last eight years," Elaine reminded him. "Don't forget that. We've got a lot to praise Him for."

"Yes, you're right," Dave agreed with a slow nod of his head.

"Besides," his wife continued, "things may just take off any time now. God is going to work everything out. Just keep on being His man."

Elaine's encouragement was medicinal in effect. It was just what her husband needed. "My wife is the one who's always been there," Dave says. "She's always stood by me, believed in me."

Elaine did not realize how true her words would prove. Athletes in Action stood on the threshhold of a remarkable surge that would dramatically multiply the impact of the ministry.

Dave would soon be leading the charge again, charting AIA's course in areas never before attempted and running headlong into obstacles never before encountered.

Had Hannah, or anyone else, been able to look just a few months ahead, he would not have believed it.

CHAPTER
FIVE

TODAY AMERICA, TOMORROW THE WORLD

"The most important thing in life is not so much where we stand, but in what direction we are moving."

Unknown

The sportswriters and broadcast journalists filed into the hotel conference room with a banter that only a sports gathering can generate. Today, there would be no typical "LAST PLACE SOX FIRE MANAGER" or NEW PLAYER SIGNS MULTI-YEAR CONTRACT" announcement. This press conference was different. The journalists realized it when the proceedings were opened with prayer. They dutifully bowed their heads, a few wondering — "Am I in the right place?"

The occasion was Athletes in Action's first public appearance in the athletic ministry's new Orange County, California, home — a "coming-out" of sorts. "We researched this area for six months before making the move here from Phoenix," Dave Hannah told his audience, which included representatives from many of the major media outlets in southern California. The AIA West team, renamed AIA USA, had made the move. (The East team would soon move to Vancouver, British Columbia to become "AIA Canada.")

Everyone knew AIA would announce the move of its team to southern California — nothing earth-shattering about that. But there were other reports: one, that a coach was to be named. Another indicated this little-known Christian organization would announce a new plan for its basketball team that could have repercussions throughout the amateur basketball world.

The journalists were dubious. Who could blame them? They had heard of Athletes in Action — a team that rarely won. Nice guys finish last.

But Hannah quickly got their attention. "Our goal is to establish ourselves as a team that can consistently defeat the best collegiate teams in the country," he said. "We want to win the National AAU Championship." It took UCLA 45 years to win its first national championship. (Granted, winning the AAU crown is less an accomplishment than winning an NCAA championship, but this was nonetheless an ambitious goal for a team that had tried and failed at several AAU tournaments.)

Hannah was just getting warmed up. "We'd like to bring some teams here and play home games at the Anaheim Convention Center. And our plan includes the development of a television network that will broadcast key games nationwide." Some in the audience may have begun wondering at this point if Hannah's imagination had gotten the best of him . . . but one thing was certain; none of their minds wandered.

Hannah went on to say that AIA would soon be sending players to the National Basketball Association (NBA). Nobody believed him, but it made quotable material for those present. The media were intrigued by these Christians: "At least they *think* big."

Then came the stopper: "Our goal, of course, is to

Brad Hoffman shoots from outside in the first Coaches' All-American game. The little guard won MVP honors in AIA's 103-88 win.

Irv Kiffin tells a packed basketball arena how Christ gave him victory over a five-year heroin addiction.

Derrick Jackson flies high against Soviets.

Derrick Jackson

AIA and Marquette players battle for the ball.

gain the greatest possible platform to share Christ. To do this, we plan to develop the best amateur basketball team in the world." This was almost too much.

"How will you know," a writer in the front interjected, "when you're the best team in the world?"

Hannah anticipated the question. "By representing the United States some day in the World Championship. Winning it will prove our point.

"Now this *is* a story," one writer thought gleefully to himself. "*Nobody* calls a press conference to announce they are going to win a national championship, much less a world championship!"

Mercifully, the journalists didn't ask how AIA planned to attain its ambitious goals. But Hannah would have been ready. He had not endured eight years of losing without picking up a few things along the way.

Why the sudden dosage of confidence for AIA? What lay behind the dramatic change in direction?

There were a number of factors, but two were fundamental to AIA's ambitious new outlook: a committed core of supporters and a new coach. The supporters were not the kind who go to basketball games to shake pom-poms and yell, though they certainly could. Instead, these were businessmen and women, who, having seen the impact of Athletes in Action, and the potential for even greater impact, decided: "Let's do something about it."

No longer would players have to miss valuable weeks of practice time while raising support. These men and women of the "Gold Medal Club," as they named the support organization, essentially volunteered to do that for the players. And the team, though still on a tight budget, would now be able to stay in hotels most of the time and get proper rest.

The financial developments were important, but

they were not the key to AIA's new plans. People were the key; only people could make plans happen. And it was going to take at least one very special man to take the lead.

Hannah had a good feeling about Coach Bill Oates. And not just because of his success story at nearby Santa Ana Junior College where he rebuilt a losing program: 10-17 and 10-18 records in his first two campaigns, to 25-6, 27-7 and 24-6 in his last three. Bill Oates is tenacious, a driver, a stickler for details, even to the point of perfectionism. But one thing stands out most about Oates — he's a winner.

After Hannah introduced him to the media, Oates said, "I'm joining Athletes in Action because of the potential it has in developing the top amateur team in the country" — ("He obviously believes it too," one writer mused) — "and our equally important goal of letting people know about our faith in Christ through athletics."

The press conference was a resounding success. Southern Californians began hearing about a new team with a unique purpose.

Dennis Beets, sports editor of the *Anaheim Bulletin,* wrote: "Athletes in Action is an organization whose activities are familiar to approximately 4,000 people — all of whom are employed by the worldwide body." But that was beginning to change; this first press conference was only the start. Now AIA had to put words into action.

Oates went to work like a whirlwind as soon as the hiring was announced. He found an assistant coach in Mike Gratzke. And daily, Oates and Hannah met to pray specifically for the players they hoped to recruit.

---

*Campus Crusade currently has over 14,000 staff in more than 150 countries.

While the coach was out talking to prospective players, Hannah was toiling to make the television broadcasts a reality. He didn't know that the TV project would soon jeopardize the very existence of the basketball team.

But right now, things looked good. Earl Dyer joined AIA to serve as director of the project. John Wooden and former NBA great, Jerry Lucas, agreed to be commentators for the 10 planned telecasts. And most exciting of all, millions of people could be reached for Christ through the unique format. Hannah put it like this: "We can talk to hundreds of thousands a year through live audiences, but we can talk to tens of millions of people a year through television."

The concept was untried: a professional, creatively done evangelistic presentation sandwiched between two halves of basketball. Some viewers automatically change the channel at the sight of a TV preacher or Christian talk show, but a basketball game is different.

TV productions can cost millions of dollars. In this case, though it was a modest $465,000, it was still an astronomical sum for AIA. But it was attainable; more than half of that amount, in fact, had already been secured. Two groups of businessmen would invest $60,000 and $100,000 respectively, Jack-In-The-Box Hamburgers would buy $15,000 in advertising and National Liberty Life planned $50,000.

The television project was a gamble and had been from the start. And it was approaching a critical stage. "Dave, there's something you need to know before we go any further with this thing," said Earl Dyer. Though he didn't want to be negative, Dyer felt this had to be said. He and Hannah were meeting in Hannah's office; it was early evening and most of the staff had gone home.

"Have you considered what would happen if for

some reason — and there are *plenty* of possible reasons — we don't get on the air? Our advertising commitments would fail but we would still owe the money invested so far. After paying that, we wouldn't have enough to pay the team's travel cost, much less the players' scholarships."

Dyer paused, giving Hannah time to digest what he had said. "What I'm saying, Dave, is this: no TV — no team. We make it here, or that's it . . . nine years down the drain."

Hannah sat stonily behind his desk, elbows on the arms of his chair, hands clasped loosely. "I understand that," he said slowly. Then the question: "Are we going to make it?"

"I don't know. Right now it looks pretty good, but we're still lacking $125,000 and time is running out . . ."

"Earl" Hannah interrupted, "we are *going* to make it. We've got to believe God for this." Dyer felt little better, and yet, Hannah sounded so sure.

After Dyer left, Hannah remained seated. He wished he were as sure as he sounded. Dave slumped down, dropping his head to his chest, and prayed.

Oates, meanwhile, was boldly putting together AIA's most challenging schedule ever. He may have done his job too well. Marquette Coach Al McGuire called it "the roughest schedule I know of. They've got one 10-day period where they play North Carolina State, Notre Dame, Cincinnati, Louisville, Alabama and Vanderbilt back-to-back," said McGuire. "The New York Knicks wouldn't want any of that."

An even greater priority, however, was recruiting the type of player who could make AIA successful with that kind of schedule.

Every few days Oates rushed into Hannah's office with the news that another player had signed. Before it was over, *every one* of the players they prayed for had come into the fold.

Included in the outstanding recruiting class: Sammy High, an all-Missouri Valley Conference player from Tulsa; Dan Knight, an all-Big 8 center from Kansas; two co-captains from Oregon State — Doug Oxsen, a 6-foot-11 center, and 6-foot-2 guard Charlie Neal; North Carolina's playmaking guard Brad Hoffman; Colorado State's Tim Hall, an all-WAC forward; and Irvin Kiffin, a 6-foot-9 forward out of Oklahoma Baptist.

People make the program. And some very special people were a part of that first Oates recruiting class. They were to be used by God in an extraordinary way.

One of those key signees was Brad Hoffman. He came reluctantly, and only for a year. It was then back to graduate school . . . or so he thought.

Brad Hoffman: *"I wanted to be the best I possibly could in everything I did."*

Brad Hoffman doesn't look like a basketball player. With a few extra pounds surrounding his midsection, the 5-foot-9, 160-pounder looks like the kid down the street who is the last chosen in sandlot pick-up games.

But Hoffman's physical deficiencies didn't keep him from becoming a co-captain and first team all-Eastern Regional choice for Dean Smith's North Carolina Tarheels as a senior. He has lots of that intangible ingredient coaches call "heart."

It was at North Carolina that Hoffman got his first exposure to Athletes in Action. He and teammates Phil Ford, Walter Davis, Tommy LaGarde, et al, trounced the AIA East team by 37 points. "AIA wasn't too impressive," Hoffman understates.

Brad had always been a winner. In junior high school he led his seventh grade team to a city championship. His love for sports was such that he would *even* go to church, something he dreaded, to remain eligible for the church team. "They put a check mark down every time you came," he says. "You had to be present twice a month to stay eligible."

"Hoffie's" competitiveness emerged early. "I wanted to be the best I possibly could in everything I did. I wanted to get straight A's in school; I wanted to be the best player on the baseball and basketball teams."

Things went pretty well for Hoffman until the summer before his senior year in high school. "My parents were divorced and the family unity that I had grown up with was suddenly gone. I was left feeling empty, though later the situation helped me find the true source of security."

Hoffman quickly realized that athletics, no matter how successful he was, could not give him the security he needed. He searched for something to fill the void in his life, until, through the influence of a Christian girlfriend who invited him to her church ("I only went to impress her"), Brad discovered what a personal relationship with Jesus Christ was all about. He invited Christ into his life. Hoffman found the source of security he was looking for, in Christ. "It doesn't last a day, a week, or a year," he learned, "but for eternity."

Two factors were especially instrumental in the young believer's spiritual growth: marriage to his girlfriend, Becky, and his involvement with the Campus Crusade movement at the University of North Carolina.

The Campus Crusade connection made it no easier for Bill Oates to overcome AIA's loser image when he

recruited the stand-out guard. But Oates was successful after he explained the ambitious commitment AIA
had made to its USA basketball program.

Another key recruit was Irvin Kiffin.

Irvin Kiffin: *"I never thought I would be an
addict. Nobody does."*

Irvin Kiffin began smoking marijuana at age 12.
He was doing heroin at 16. By age 20, he had been an
addict for five years, stood 6-foot-8 and weighed a
gaunt 160 lbs.

"I first started doing drugs because I wanted to be
a part of the group," says Kiffin. "In my neighbor-
hood, there were two sides of the fence. On one was
the 'hip' or 'in-crowd,' and on the other, what we
called 'creeps' or 'yo-yos.'

"All you had to do was smoke a little marijuana,
drink a little wine, and have a young lady on your
arm, and you were accepted by the group. I never
thought I would be an addict," says Kiffin. "Nobody
does."

Somehow — even now he doesn't know how —
Kiffin managed to play one year of basketball at
Springfield Gardens High School. He first learned the
game where some of the toughest street ball is played,
and unlike a lot of kids on the playground, he received
a scholarship to play basketball in college.

"I first enrolled at Virginia Union University in
1969," he says. "But because I used drugs, I wasn't
able to contribute to the team in any great capacity. I
couldn't play ball unless I was high."

Unable to study, Kiffin failed most of his courses
and flunked out — twice. After dropping out the
second time he was at an all-time low. "I went back to
New York and just hung out on the corner, getting my

heroin where I could."

About that time "Kiff" began spending time with a girl, Myra, who later became his wife. Myra gave him an ultimatum: "Kiff, I love you," she said. "But if you continue using drugs, we don't have a future together."

Kiffin agreed to try a rehabilitation center. It took only three weeks to overcome the physical dependence, but he was far from overcoming the psychological dependence. "My security had been in the group and in drugs before, but now it turned to my wife."

He almost lost Myra the day he married her when he shot up on their wedding night. But the next day, with things a little smoothed over, they left for Oklahoma Baptist University where God changed his life.

"At Oklahoma Baptist I began to notice something different about one of my teammates, Wardell Jeffries. He had something that I didn't have, a certain peace about him and he handled situations differently than most people."

"It's Jesus Christ in my life," Jeffries explained. "He's given me peace and purpose in my life."

Kiffin knew immediately that he wanted Jesus in his life. "I wanted that peace, "he said, "but at first I was confused because as far as I was concerned, only 'creeps' went to church and 'yo-yos' believed in God. But I realized it was God working in my life that brought me through my earlier crisis.

"It was then that I opened my heart to Jesus Christ and accepted Him as my Savior and Lord. Jesus filled the void that I had tried to fill with everything else. If I hadn't found Christ, I think I'd be back in New York, messing around, in jail, or maybe even dead."

Kiffin went on to earn honorable mention all-American honors at OBU, averaging 18 points and 10

rebounds a game. Oates heard about him and recruited the forward, now 6-foot-9 and a healthy 220
lbs. Kiffin was now ready to use his skills to tell others
what Christ had done in his life.

A third special person was Tim Hall.

Tim Hall: *"I wasn't used to failure."*

Tim Hall's preconceived notion about Bill Oates
wasn't even close. "I thought I would meet a
boisterous type of guy who would really sell the
program," Hall said later. "But he was soft-spoken,
almost timid." The two got together at a prearranged
meeting in a Denver hotel, an hour south of Ft. Collins
where Hall was finishing up his senior year at
Colorado State University.

"I can remember him looking me in the eye," Hall
continued, "and saying, 'I think you can be a great
part of this team.' " Hall signed, and would later
become one of the stalwart spiritual leaders on the
team.

The Grand Junction, Colo. native came to know
Christ as a freshman in college. He remembers well
the circumstances surrounding his decision. "I walked
into the lunchroom one day and saw my roommate
sitting there. He said, 'Hey, Hall, I enrolled you for a
Bible study class — you need it!'"

"I couldn't argue with him," Tim says. "I had
come to the point where I was frustrated and worried;
frustrated with basketball and worried about my
grades. I wasn't used to failure. For the first time in
my life I was faced with problems I didn't have
answers for."

The Bible study group went on a hayride one night
and Hall went along, having heard that a steak fry was
included. It was at the outing that he first learned how
he could know God personally.

"A guy stood up and shared what Christ had done in his life," Hall says. "This guy's life had been more messed up than mine, although his life had changed to the point where he could joke about his former ways now.

"He was saying, 'Man, I wanted to commit suicide but I couldn't jump out the window because I lived on the first floor, and I couldn't cut my wrists because I used an electric razor.' He finished by quoting John 1:12 — 'But as many as received Him, to them He gave the right to become children of God . . .'

"I knew I was ready," Tim said. He prayed a simple prayer, asking Christ to come into his life, on that cold Colorado night.

Christ didn't immediately solve all his problems — for Hall, in fact, the Christian life raised a new problem that he as an athlete would soon be forced to deal with.

Oates had his team. The entire Athletes in Action ministry anticipated the start of the season which promised to be AIA's greatest and most fruitful ever. It would be another year before the two great centers, Ralph Drollinger and Bayard Forrest, were added to the roster, but Oates knew this team could win.

Living up to expectations, AIA jumped out to a fast start, winning its first six games. Even the team's first loss, an 83-82 heartbreaker to powerful North Carolina State, indicated that some changes had indeed occurred. That was apparent to N.C. State Coach Norm Sloan who observed, "We played an excellent basketball team tonight. That's not the same Athletes in Action team we usually play. They obviously knew what we were doing."

But this team had not arrived yet. There was still one critical lesson to learn; it showed in anger and conflict within the team. It was to be a painful lesson.

GOD IS YOUR AUDIENCE

"Show me a good loser and I'll show you a loser."

Leo Durocher
Former Baseball Manager

Bill Oates' eyes were fiery. His steely glare swept the locker room. Nobody spoke.

The "new" AIA USA basketball team had just lost its second game in four tries against Division I competition. Not bad by early AIA standards, but Oates knew this team was better. Tonight's game was not a defeat — it was an embarrassment.

The opponent, Purdue University, traditionally fields excellent basketball teams, but the 1975-76 edition was certainly not a great team. AIA could no longer blame defeats like this 99-80 shellacking on a dearth of talent. There was another ingredient still missing and Oates thought he knew what it was.

"You guys didn't give much of an effort," he half-shouted through clenched teeth. "Your effort stunk!" Oates called a team meeting for later that night before storming angrily out of the locker room.

"I thought he was going to kill us," breathed a relieved Tim Hall.

The players quietly gathered in a dorm room an hour later. "Let's sing a song," said Bible study leader John Sears. "Let's sing 'Amazing Grace.' "

Oates and some of the players, particularly the new ones, were in no mood to sing. "I can't sing now," the coach snapped. "You guys stunk out there."

Oates' blunt, though honest, appraisal of the team's performance was a catalyst for a lengthy discussion that went far into the night. The interaction between the team members solved nothing, but did define the problem: two distinctly different schools of thought existed on how important winning was to the success of the ministry. Something had to be done.

AIA's next game was against No. 8 ranked University of Cincinnati, a powerful team enjoying its basketball heyday.

Broadcaster Dave Iverson put the situation in perspective: "Having lost to Purdue by 19 points, we could expect to lose to Cincinnati by 30 or 35."

Hannah was in Ann Arbor, Michigan, at the time for a speaking engagement at University of Michigan football team chapel service. The AIA Director had a troubled mind as well.

The television project had suffered a series of setbacks so incredible that they seemed satanic in design. First, Notre Dame and Indiana both cancelled their games with AIA, ". . . the first time in eight years an opponent has pulled out," Hannah noted. The number of broadcasts had to be reduced from ten to eight (eventually to six, due to costs).

Several cameras broke down during the North Carolina State game and the AIA network lost the exciting overtime contest. Cincinnati was chosen as the substitute game. The rearranged schedule conflicted with Jerry Lucas' and the commentator had to drop out. The personnel and scheduling changes, in turn, combined to hurt AIA's already shaky credibility with independent TV stations. "When it rains it pours," Hannah thought.

It rained harder. Several of the businessmen who had collectively pledged $160,000 failed to come through with their pledges. Then the "Jack-In-The-Box" $15,000 fell through. Suddenly a large portion of the committed money had vanished. "Lord, are you leading us in this," Hannah wondered, "or did I read you wrong?"

The most disconcerting news was that Mizlou, the TV syndicator, had only 35% of the U.S. market cleared: "We just can't clear your product," they said.

If $125,000 in additional advertising was not sold soon, there might not be an Athletes in Action.

Hannah knew he needed to get his mind off the TV crisis. He decided to call Oates to find out how the team fared against Purdue.

Oates told Hannah the bad news, and then added, "We've got a problem, Dave. It seems like some of the guys don't think it matters too much if we win or not. They feel like the important thing is not blowing their cool on the court and presenting the message at halftime, and, they're right, of course, but . . ."

Both men agreed that presenting the gospel was the central purpose of Athletes in Action. No question there. But they also understood the importance of winning.

"People are more likely to be open to our message if we're successful," Oates said. And Hannah knew from experience that what the coach was saying was true.

"Dave," Oates continued, "they were saying things like, 'It doesn't really matter whether we win or not, as long as we give our best for God.' That's true. But how can we have a better team than Purdue, get beat by 20 points and then say we'd given our best? We're just not playing aggressively enough to win."

The TV project hung in the balance. Nobody will sponsor the telecasts of a team that always loses. Only the most sadistic of the nation's sports fans would enjoy such a spectacle. "Hey, that Christian team is on again," they'd say. "Let's see how bad they get beat this time."

Hannah understood the urgency of the issue. "I'll try to help," he told Oates. Hannah called Wendell Deyo, AIA's staff member in Cincinnati who specializes in a ministry with the city's pro athletes, and explained the situation. "Try to get them to understand from a biblical perspective what it *really* means to do your best," Hannah told Deyo, and then he told him to expect a call from Oates.

Hannah could still feel anxiety for the TV project tightening around him. He sat back on the bed in his hotel room and opened his Bible to Matthew 14, the passage where Jesus is walking on the water. Hannah saw something in the passage that leaped out at him.

"Peter actually began walking on the water toward Christ," Hannah says, "but then he got into problems. When he noticed how hard the wind was blowing and how high the waves were, he took his eyes off Christ. And when he took his eyes off Christ, he began to sink.

"Although I heard no voice out loud, it was as if God was speaking directly to me. 'Dave,' he said, 'you've done the same thing. During the last few weeks you've had one problem after another. But the real problem is that you've taken your eyes off me.'

"And I really had. I kept looking at all these problems and saying, 'What incredible thing is going to happen next?' But now as I thought about it, nothing had happened to actually destroy the TV project. I had allowed these problems to become giants.

"As I read the passage, the Lord gave me a peace

that he was taking care of the project. He was saying to me, 'Dave, I'm in control. Don't worry about it.' "

Oates called Deyo at noon. "Never before have I not known what to do," he said, with obvious emotion. "These guys don't think winning is important. I think winning is important," he said slowly. "Do you?"

Deyo assured the coach that he did, and he promised to speak to the team. Deyo arrived at the team's hotel just before three o'clock. He found the entire traveling party crammed into one of the player's rooms — on the floor, tucked into corners, sprawled across the beds. A few stood. There was barely room to move.

Deyo's concern was that the players recognize there is a tremendous dimension to winning — expansive media coverage, for example — that they had failed to recognize. "You've only been looking at winning from *your* perspective," he said, "not from the perspective of the people who stay behind in the city to have their ministry.

"When people around here come up to me in the next few days they're not going to ask me if you were nice guys on the court. They're going to ask, 'Who won?' And when they hear that *you* won, they're going to say, 'You guys beat U.C.?! That's pretty good.' They're going to be impressed, and that opens doors for our ministry here.

"I don't want to be apologizing for you people when you leave here. I want to say, 'Yeah, I'm a part of that.' "

The speaker sensed that the players' minds were clicking. A couple of them shifted nervously, but their attention never wavered.

Deyo then shifted his focus to Scripture. "In Romans 12:1,2 Paul is enjoining the believers in Rome to 'present your bodies a living and holy sacrifice.' " He reminded them of the sacrifices that the Israelites made in the Old Testament: "They gave the very best they had and sacrificed it. Paul is urging us to do the same thing, but he is urging us to give our very lives and bodies. Deyo paused for what seemed like a long time, his gaze spanning the room.

"You guys want to worship God?" he asked rhetorically. Another pause. "You're basketball players — the more aggressive you play, the more intensity you play with — the louder you are saying thank you to God.

"Every one of you has something to be thankful for. You can either whisper it, say it out loud, or you can shout it. But ask yourselves, 'How loud am I saying thank you to God through my performance?' "

When Deyo was finished, everyone was quiet and reflective. Something had gotten through to them, but nobody, including Deyo, was sure what it was. The answer would come that night.

Oates thanked Deyo, and as the speaker turned to leave he felt a hand on his shoulder. He turned and looked up into the face of Tim Hall. "Wendell," Hall said, "I want to thank you for coming. I needed to hear that." The 6-foot-8 forward realized that he had slipped into a nonaggressive style of play, subconsciously thinking it would somehow distinguish him as a Christian athlete.

They shook hands and Deyo told him, "You can expect to win tonight, Tim."

Coach Gale Catlett's University of Cincinnati Bearcats were always a bear at home: they'd won 33 consecutive contests in the antiquated Armory Fieldhouse. Every one of Cincinnati's starters returned from the 1974-75 team that had posted a 23-6 record, and Bearcat fans were expecting greater things as they awaited the opener with AIA. The Athletes in Action team could hear the boisterous throng even when inside the visitors' locker room, located beneath the cavernous arena.

During introductions, a spotlight followed the Bearcats as they trotted across the red, white and black carpet that had been laid on the floor of the darkened arena. Their guards stood 6-foot-4 and 6-foot-5, a hefty height advantage over AIA who answered with 6-foot-1 Eldon Lawyer, in his first start of the year, and 5-foot-9 Hoffman.

But the small guards were instrumental in getting AIA off to a good start. In the opening minutes Hoffman hit Kiffin twice on long "alley-oop" passes, giving the muscular forward a pair of easy baskets. His teammates got the message: "We can play with these guys!"

Hall was working hard too, on both ends of the court. Fighting for position, he clawed and scrapped his way to seven first half rebounds.

"The guy's an animal," someone near the Cincinnati bench said to a friend. "These guys are supposed to be Christians?" His friend nodded in agreement, but both knew they admired the quality that characterized Hall's play — intensity. That same quality marked the entire AIA team. Either Deyo's talk had made a difference or some other basketball team had slipped into AIA's uniforms before the game.

Lawyer had 12 points by halftime, helping his team to a 41-33 lead. The strategy session at intermission was quick and to the point. "Intensity!" some of the players shouted as they made their way out of the locker room.

"Remember who you're representing out there," someone yelled as the teams lined up for the second half tip-off. But tonight, no reminder was needed.

The final score was 86-81, a tribute to potent fast-

breaking, excellent ball-handling and all-around intense play. This team now knew what intensity and
total effort meant, and they didn't intend to forget it.

The victory was perhaps sweetest for Tim Hall.
"Until this game," he said, "I guess I'd forgotten that
basketball fans like to see you play hard. In the years
since I'd accepted Christ I had become sort of a 'wet
pup.' I was so unaggressive because I was afraid I
might offend somebody by my play on the court.

"But when I realized that a Christian can play
aggressively, I decided to go all out each day, in every
practice and game. And if that means diving for a
loose ball or clawing for a rebound, that's what I'm
going to do.

"Ultimately," he summarizes, "I'm accountable to
God. God is my audience and He wants my best
effort."

While Iverson was finishing up his broadcast by
calling the win "the greatest all-time victory for
Athletes in Action," one key person still did not know
the outcome of the game. Dave Hannah, in fact, had
"sort of forgotten about the game" while speaking to a
very responsive audience at the University of Michigan that night.

"Suddenly, though," he said, "I realized that the
game was over in Cincinnati, and my heart skipped a
couple of beats. I tried not to expect a 30-point loss as
I called up Wendell Deyo. I reminded myself that God
was in control, whatever the outcome."

"Dave, it was a great game," Wendell said from the
phone in his kitchen.

"Immediately I felt much better, " Hannah recalls.
"Although I didn't know who had won, at least I knew
we had played a respectable game. I guess Wendell
assumed I already knew the score. Anyhow, he just
went on, saying things like 'It was a close game,' and

'It was so exciting,' and 'There was a great crowd.'

"Finally, I said, 'Great, Wendell, but *who won?*' He said, "We won.' I said, 'We what? We won? We actually won the game?' When he said, 'Oh, yeah, we won by five points,' I was stunned. The Lord had promised to take care of our needs, but I hadn't expected this.

"I couldn't have been more thrilled. After the Purdue game I had gone to bed thinking the TV project was almost dead, but now I saw it revived. Instead of showing a loss to N.C. State on TV, we had a win over a better team. I had new enthusiasm to go out and sell advertising and negotiate with stations."

Hannah put his renewed zest to use. He and Dyer flew to Los Angeles, Philadelphia, New York, Chicago, Detroit, St. Louis and Pittsburgh in one week. These major markets were cleared but the *major* hurdle was not — the advertising remained unsold.

The days turned into weeks, but still nothing.

"They're really gambling on the TV deal," Century City sports marketing specialist Max Muhleman told a *Los Angeles Times* reporter. "They're buying time for basketball games . . . and showing them on a 60-day delay basis. It's a tough sell."[1] The syndicating company working with AIA recommended that the entire project be dropped. But commitments had been made; it was too late to back out.

All of the TV games had to be played, taped, edited and sent to the stations by January 22, halfway through the team's season. Christmas arrived, and still, not one dollar of advertising had sold. With businesses closed for the holidays, potential sponsors could not even consider the project until after the first week in January.

Dave spent Christmas with his family, unable to do anything about the looming crisis. He knew his credibility was in jeopardy . . . as was the entire Athletes in Action ministry.

"It got to the point where I didn't even want to think about it," Hannah says. "But I was prepared for whatever God wanted."

THE ROAD HOME

"If Christ had been a basketball player, He'd have played with great intensity. He did everything in His life all out."

Bayard Forrest

It's been said that God is seldom early, but never late. To that, Dave Hannah nowadays says a hearty "amen." But just days before the advertising deadline, sales efforts were still getting nowhere.

"You're too unknown and too late," advertisers maintained. Hannah's hopes were fading fast.

"I just can't believe God has allowed the project to come this far to let it die, " he said to Dyer.

Dave did manage to get an appointment with the public relations director of a national car manufacturing company. "This may be another waste of time," he thought, "but it can't hurt . . ."

He showed an audiovisual presentation and did his best to explain the merits of the AIA proposal. "I then mustered up enough courage to ask for two minutes of advertising at $75,000."

The P.R. director turned to his marketing man and said, "Let's buy it."

"I almost fell out of my seat!" Hannah recalls. After six months of struggling, half of the project's advertising had sold in one 45-minute appointment. And several days later, two additional slots sold for $16,000 and $20,000. The project was saved! Hannah's faith had undergone another stretching as he saw God provide at the last moment.

The team completed its 1975-76 season with a best-ever 37-8 won/lost mark, climaxed by a season-ending National AAU Championship. But Hannah knew this was no time to relax and grow complacent; he wanted to continue living on the edge of faith.

Not surprisingly, AIA staff barely had time to breath a collective sigh of relief over the TV situation before tackling another challenge. Despite advice from many to the contrary, AIA planned to follow through with its intention to sponsor home basketball games.

Staff members talked with a number of the area's top promotion and media experts, and the response was generally the same. One executive, though sympathetic to AIA and its cause, did his best to talk Hannah, AIA P.R. Director Greg Hicks and others, out of the plan. "You've got no money, no alumni and no student body to draw from. Who's going to come to your home games?"

Few locations would present greater competition in the sports/entertainment market. Southern California is home for ten professional sports teams, better than a dozen basketball playing universities and a myriad of other sporting possibilities that range from 100-plus racquetball clubs to sailboat racing. AIA, not a college and not a pro team, but an amateur team in a class of its own, had created a mammoth task for itself.

"It *can* be done," a few advisors said. "But it will take an extraordinary amount of work."

"We'll never know until we try," Hannah argued.

The next step was one of faith; two top basketball schools — the University of San Francisco and

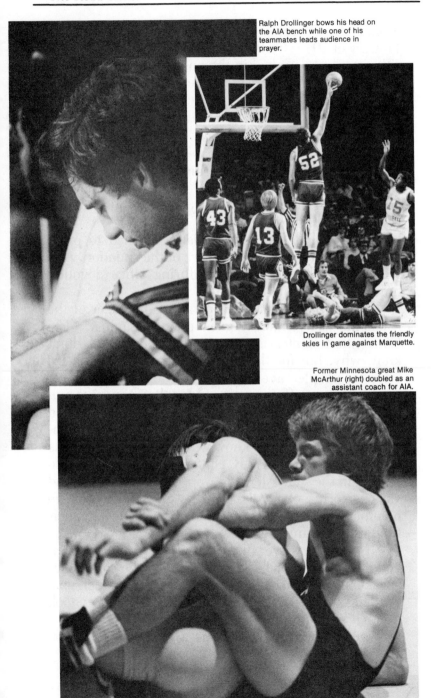

Ralph Drollinger bows his head on the AIA bench while one of his teammates leads audience in prayer.

Drollinger dominates the friendly skies in game against Marquette.

Former Minnesota great Mike McArthur (right) doubled as an assistant coach for AIA.

Nevada Las Vegas — were scheduled for contests in January of 1977. Staff began praying that both universities would be ranked in the polls at the time of their games with AIA. "If we can get two Top-20 ranked teams in here, "Hicks pointed out, "a lot more people are going to be interested *and* hear the players speak."

Shortly thereafter, Oates walked into Hannah's office with bad news. "We can't get the Convention Center for the San Francisco game," he said. "The Ice Capades Show has it booked." This was bad news indeed; there would obviously be no home game without a facility.

Hannah and Oates immediately paused to pray, asking God to somehow take care of the situation. AIA staff joined the prayer effort during office devotion times.

Several days later, the operations manager of the Anaheim Convention Center phoned saying, "The Convention Center is yours on January 20. I don't know why, but for the first time in 12 years the Ice Capades people have cancelled."

The prayer effort continued for the opponents and for ticket sales. The public relations staff worked vigorously to promote the home games. "The frightening thing is, none of us know what we're doing," Hicks candidly admitted. A P.R. conference was arranged to help train the staff. Men and women in advertising and various forms of media-related work, some of them members of the Gold Medal Club, volunteered their time in the training effort.

"Nobody has ever filled that arena (Anaheim Convention Center) for basketball," one of the conference speakers noted. The statement served as a personal challenge to each of the P.R. staff members. They took a "we'll see" attitude.

The department worked as a team. Each person

was assigned the responsibility of promoting the USF game in one Orange County city in addition to his regular responsibilities.

Posters went up in sporting goods stores, thousands of flyers were inserted in local church bulletins. Jack-In-The-Box Hamburgers agreed to insert a flyer with each order sold. Local newspapers and broadcast media were contacted. The *Los Angeles Times* posed the key question in the headline of one story: "AIA AT HOME, ANYBODY CARE?"

Tickets began to sell. God was answering prayer, including dramatic answers for the upcoming opponents, as the staff would see.

Meanwhile, the basketball team was doing its part by winning. The team blitzed through a preseason exhibition tour of Australia, running up a perfect record in 18 games. Lindsay Gaze, head of Australia's amateur Basketball Federation said, "The Athletes in Action USA basketball team is far and above the best team to ever come to Australia."

Many of the crowds were not as responsive to the gospel in Australia as the team had hoped, but Tim Hall will never forget one man who was. "I sat down on the bench after a game with a midget who had deformed hands," he said, "and when I explained that God loved him and had a plan for his life, he began to cry.

"His father had died and his mother was an alcoholic, but when he realized that God still loved him, it had a strong impact on him. When he prayed and received Jesus Christ as his Savior you could see an immediate change."

The team initially struggled when the collegiate portion of its schedule began. Part of the slow start could be attributed to adaptations as the team adjusted to new personnel, including centers Bayard Forrest and Ralph Drollinger of UCLA. The two, however, at last remedied the weakness AIA had suffered so long at the post position.

Drollinger, and 6-foot-10 Forrest from Arizona's Grand Canyon College, both turned down NBA opportunities: the former returned a Boston Celtics contract offer unopened when it arrived postage due, and Forrest refused a $230,000, two-year offer by the Seattle Supersonics.

The AIA big men also adjusted to "playing together" off the court. Drollinger and tall teammate Doug Oxen found a unique way to answer the frequent queries about their height *and* provide an avenue to talk about Christ. Standing together in hotel lobbies and airports, they wait for the inevitable question: "How tall are you guys?"

"Six-foot-eleven, goin' to heaven," Oxen deadpans.

"Seven-foot-two, how 'bout you?" adds Drollinger.

On another road trip the joke was on Drollinger. Sharing a meal with some of the players, Coach Oates asked his rookie center to wave when he went to talk with a waitress. "She wants to know which of you is the 7-foot-2 guy from UCLA," Oates said. In actuality, Oates told the waitress which one would pay the bill.

Ralph waved, Oates left, and the gullible rookie got stuck with both bills.

An intense style of play continued to characterize the team, and AIA began to generate new respect from opponents. One opposing player publicly questioned if the Christian team could "handle it when people play a little rough." By the second half of the game, however, AIA's tough play not only removed his doubts but left him frustrated. "I'm not going to play against these Christians!" he said in exasperation. He asked his father, the head coach, to remove him from the lineup.

The player, who had labeled Christianity a "crutch" for weak people, began to consider the faith from a new perspective. Like many others, he had not rejected Christ, but a false picture of Christianity. He later invited Christ into his life.

AIA's tough style of play was essential for success in big-time basketball where the "survival of the fittest" principle applies. Basketball, though officially a "non-contact" sport, becomes very rough at times. And AIA players "mix it up" with the best of them — just ask head trainer Ed Gold. He treats the injuries that are the by-product of a reckless, rough-and-tumble style of play.

"One season," Gold says, "Hoffman severely sprained an ankle twice, played half the year with a hernia which later required surgery and had to see a specialist about a poke he got in the eye."

But another player, Steve Copp, gets the Purple Heart. Copp kept Gold busy single-handedly: "He broke his nose, lost a tooth, suffered a severe groin pull, pulled a hamstring, sprained his ankle and had bone chips in his ankle. "Then," Gold adds, "to top it all off, he sat down on the bench too hard and broke his tailbone!"

A second factor in AIA's success stems from unselfish team play. With a focus on Christ, and not "self," the Athletes in Action team has not often suffered internal problems. They recall Philippians 2:3, which says "Do nothing from selfishness or empty conceit, but with humility of mind let each of you regard one another as more important than himself."

But even Christian teams are not immune to the effects of "self." Some members of the AIA team were once murmuring that they deserved a larger proportion of the 200 minutes (5 players X 40 minutes) of playing time each game.

Coach Oates thought of a solution. He sat them down after practice one day and gave each athlete a piece of paper. "Write down how many minutes you think you ought to be playing," he told them. A quick count showed that the players' "recommendations" totaled over 350 minutes!

Oates, half-smiling, chided them, "Should we sneak three extra people out there and hope the other team doesn't notice?"

The players got the message; *somebody* has to sit on the bench!

Before returning to California for its first-ever home game, the team stopped in Hastings, Nebraska and put a 116-70 pasting on undermanned Hastings College. During their stay, Tim Hall walked into his hotel room one evening and found roommate Drollinger stripped to his shorts, running in place. Ralph was working hard, sweat rolling off his body.

Hall, barely controlling his amusement at the sight, said, "Ralph, what are you doing?!"

"I'm getting ready for the San Francisco game," Ralph replied, still running. "This is a big game." Drollinger stopped now, resting his hands on his hips while he caught his breath. As he looked at his teammate, the atmosphere changed. Now Hall grew reflective as well. There was no more joking.

"God is going to use this game," Ralph said. "And we're going to win it."

After nine years and 365 consecutive road games, the stage was set. Athletes in Action was coming home.

CHAPTER EIGHT

HALLELUJAH WHAT A TEAM!

"They beat you up in the first half, pray for you at halftime, then beat you up in the second half."

Jerry Tarkanian
Head Coach, Nevada Las Vegas

Athletes in Action's Irvin Kiffin soared high over the basket, catching the pass in mid-flight, and with a snap of both wrists slammed the ball through the net for two more points.

The partisan crowd roared its approval, a foreign but welcome sound to a team playing its first-ever home game. One could hardly have blamed the AIA players had they paused a moment to enjoy the unfamiliar sound.

After all, there were people here, almost 7,000, a near-capacity crowd for the Anaheim Convention Center.

"How 'bout it, Ed?" one of the players said to trainer Ed Gold, taking a quick panoramic glance at the packed arena as they sat together on the AIA bench.

"Unbelievable," Gold muttered as both quickly riveted their attention back to the action before them.

The promotional efforts had paid off. The majority of the fans probably came out for one of two reasons: one, curiosity, and two, to see the other team play.

Coach Bob Gaillard brought his University of San

Francisco team to the Anaheim Convention Center riding high with a perfect 19-0 record that put them at the very pinnacle of collegiate basketball with a firm grip on the No. 1 spot in both wire service polls. Led by super-sophomore center Bill Cartwright, the Dons had rolled over national powers like Tennessee, Utah, Arizona State and Houston (twice).

Houston coach Guy Lewis told Gaillard after the second defeat, "You're devastating. If you guys improve any more, you'll be chewing up the NBA."[1]

A week before heading south to Anaheim, USF played Pepperdine, the team expected to be its chief rival for the West Coast Athletic Conference Championship. San Francisco won the game, 107-72. A sign in the stands that night said it best: "The Dons Are Awesome."

Gaillard had assembled the bulk of his powerhouse two years before by pulling a recruiting coup, landing a freshman class consisting of prep all-Americans Cartwright, 6-foot-8 James Hardy of Long Beach and Oklahoma City's 6-foot-6 Winfred Boynes. It took an estimated 50 visits to Long Beach to land Hardy, but the battle for Boynes was even more intense. It came down to a two-man dogfight — Gaillard and Louis-ville's Denny Crum.

Boynes, strangely enough, said that hand slaps did it. "I couldn't give five to Coach Crum," he said. "I could to Coach Gaillard."[2]

Later, at the end of the 1976-77 season, Bob Gaillard would be named Coach of the Year. But for Gaillard, Coach of the Year might be a misnomer. Psychiatrist of the Year seems more accurate.

He later described his team as "psychos" and "mentally imbalanced" after a season in which the Coach of the Year did more counseling than coaching. One can hardly blame him: "He spent the evening before one game trying to talk Hardy, his 'eccentric genius' of a sophomore forward, into playing. Hardy, never sure how much basketball means to him, has said he might be happier 'living in a treehouse back in Alabama.'

"Marlon Redmond, the senior 'leader,' walked out of a midseason practice and brought his mother back a couple of days later to iron things out. 'Everything was too crazy,' he explained. 'The young guys needed someone to get their attention.'

"Soph guard Winford Boynes, the 'loner,' loves to practice — from about 3-4:30 a.m. The night watchman was alerted."[3]

Though in need of a team psychiatrist, USF lacked nothing in talent.

The only Don superstar to miss the contest was Hardy who sustained a knee sprain in practice the week before the game.

Though entirely healthy, the Christian team was nevertheless an unlikely candidate to knock off the kingpin of college basketball. Unlike USF, AIA had lost some games — six to be exact — against the likes of Marquette, Minnesota, North Carolina and Oregon.

But now the game had begun and records no longer mattered. San Francisco moved ahead 15-14 with 12:44 left in the first half when Cartwright hit a five-footer in front of the basket. A San Francisco lead was no surprise — few people believed that the two teams even belonged on the same court.

"Push him to the middle, Timmy!" Oates shouted to Hall as his forward defensed the super-quick Boynes.

Dave Hannah had one of the choice seats in the arena, a fold-up chair at courtside. He couldn't help but overhear some comments made by two men seated near him.

"Oh, San Francisco is just toying with them," one man said to his friend. "In a little while they'll blow them out."

Hannah paid little attention, but screamed, "**De**-fense! **De**-fense! **De**-fense" every time his team came to their end of the floor.

The din inside the arena grew louder when, suddenly, just over three minutes after Cartwright's basket, AIA went up by 10 points, 27-17.

The surge brought an excited Oates to his feet . . . but he still refused to relinquish the "worry towel" that he invariably clutched in his hand during a game.

AIA managed to maintain its lead throughout the first half. The buzzer sounded with AIA holding a 49-38 lead and nearly 7,000 disbelieving fans shaking their heads.

As the San Francisco team shuffled to the locker room to plot its comeback, the AIA players returned to their bench. The lone exception was Hoffman who trotted to the scorer's table, took the public address microphone and walked out to center court.

The crowd grew suddenly subdued, listening intently as Hoffman began to speak. Most of the fans had heard of AIA's special halftime presentation — the thrust of what is probably basketball's most unique halftime "show."

Becky Hoffman, seven months pregnant, watched from the stands and prayed a brief, silent prayer as her husband began.

Hoffman spoke from his heart. He candidly shared how the divorce of his parents shook him badly during his childhood.

"I wandered aimlessly for a long time without much direction, searching for something — I wasn't sure quite what — to give my life some meaning." The audience grew more subdued. The halftime hubbub of noisy small talk, people moving to and from the concessions and restrooms, was strangely missing.

"I think everyone searches for security in one form or another — financial or peace of mind or whatever," the 6-foot-9 floor leader said. "I found my security and I found *myself* on September 13,1970. That's the day I asked Jesus Christ to come into my life."

Freeman Blade, the 6-foot-2 guard from Eastern Montana College, followed Hoffman to the mike. *L.A. Times* columnist John Hall described Blade: "as polished as any Shakespearean actor as he gave a dramatic rendition treating the history of Christ's life."

One man at the game paid special attention at halftime. After hearing the testimonies, he decided to rededicate his life to Christ. The next week he told his boss he'd stolen $100 from the company. Surprised at the man's courageous confession, the employer told him to donate the money to AIA. More than 100 people had indicated on cards that they had received Christ as a result of the presentation.

Afterward, the Athletes in Action squad made its belated departure to the locker room and conducted a hurried strategy session, consisting mostly of "let's keep doing what we're doing."

Coach Oates seldom dwelled on the positive at halftime. Time didn't allow. Instead, he gave a capsule discourse on what needed correction.

"Pressure them on defense," he said. "Push the ball down the floor. Cartwright is having a great game; we've got to stop him."

Moments before the second half opened Drollinger and Forrest reminded each other of their own plan to stop the San Francisco center.

"I'll wear him out; you put him away," Forrest said to his battery-mate before taking the court. "I'm gonna go as hard as I can and I'm gonna put my fist up to signal you to come in, Ralph — then you go as hard as you can, then put your fist up."

San Francisco's comeback never materialized. Hoffman hit his running mate, Lawyer, with a quick pass off a fastbreak for the first two points of the half and AIA never looked back. Everyone in the arena watched incredulously as the AIA lead widened to what seemed an impossible 20 points 10 minutes later.

Hannah noticed that the man seated near him had a different attitude now. "You know, this team is incredible," he said.

It was a very physical second half of play. One USF player left the game with an injury and Hoffman probably should have done the same when he was knocked to the floor and stepped on, injuring a rib.

One sports writer took note of the Christian team's tough play. After "viewing the 'church-going do-gooders' for the first time," he was "startled by how intense and tough they are once they get into uni-form."[4]

Drollinger replaced Forrest for the second time with less than eight minutes remaining. San Francisco's doom was sealed soon thereafter. An exhausted Cartwright asked to be taken out and with him went what remained of the Don's rapidly deteriorating offense. Forrest and Drollinger exchanged a knowing look.

The San Francisco seven-footer pumped in 27 points on the night, but he was more than neutralized on the boards by AIA's one-two tandem at center. Forrest had 14 rebounds to Cartwright's seven, while Drollinger chipped in 18 points.

The final 19-point margin (104-85) was no surprise; the surprise was the team with the higher point total.

As Marlon Redmond, one of USF's starters, was walking off the court he was asked if AIA was the best club his team had faced. He responded with an "are you kidding me?" look, then said, "By far."[5]

One California writer summed it up best: "The dashing Dons, otherwise unbeaten, are still trying to figure out what struck them and which way their dash went."[6]

The most ecstatic people in the arena were probably the AIA support staff who toiled so hard to make the game happen.

Ticket Manager Ron McLain phoned his hometown sports editor in Yakima, Washington bubbling over with the news.

"We just beat San Francisco!"

"Who the *$¢%* do you have playing for you?!" came the response.

Sports Information Director B.B. Branton got a similar response when he called in the results to the Associated Press.

"You just beat San Francisco?" said the AP writer. "you've got to be kidding!" Branton made the writer a believer and the story went out over the wire into newsrooms all over the country.

Branton couldn't contain his excitement; his hometown sports editor had to hear the news too. Sam Heys, sports editor for the *Columbus (*GA*) Enquirer and Ledger,* told the story two days later in a column: "When you wake up to a ringing telephone at 2 a.m., you figure somebody's had a baby, somebody's died, or somebody's in jail. But Thursday night, it was just a case of somebody winning a basketball game.

"I stumbled to the phone forewarned that it was my fanatical sports friend from California. Maybe he had a hot scoop; the Yankees had traded Reggie Jackson to the Dodgers. I said, 'Hello,' and the immediate yelp was, 'We beat San Francisco.'

"San Francisco? All the San Franciscos I've ever known quickly raced through my still-sleeping mind. The Seals? The Giants? How about the 49ers? Then suddenly it came to me: the nation's No. 1 college basketball team. Everybody's heard of the Dons. 'That's pretty good,' I muttered."[7]

Meanwhile, at courtside, Hannah and the players were surrounded by a post-game throng of inquisitive media. Hannah put the victory in the perspective of a 10-year effort. "Everyone thinks we're an overnight sensation," he said. "They don't realize that the success we saw here tonight came from 10 years of work and prayer.

"Good things don't come easily," he added. "Sometimes Christians think all you have to do is pray once or twice." And referring to AIA's successful TV network, he said, "Tonight we not only beat the No.1 team in the nation, but we're going to show it to a few million people."

The media was impressed. NBC-TV's *Grandstand* carried action footage from the game. *Sports Illustrated* scheduled a special story titled, "Hallelujah, What a Team!" The startling upset made headlines in daily newspapers across the country as Athletes in Action moved from the obscurity of the sports score lists to glaring headlines and full-scale features. Writers wanted to know what this team was about.

And yet, some remained skeptical. "A fluke," they said. "After all, Hardy was out and any team can have a good night."

Just nine days later Athletes in Action had the opportunity to again prove itself when the University of Nevada-Las Vegas came to town. Ranked 5th by AP, owners of a sparkling 16-1 record and a 100-plus points per game scoring average, Jerry Tarkanian's

Myra Kittin (left) and Becky Hoffman are husbands' biggest supporters.

Tim Hall (50) battles for a jump ball in AIA-USSR clash in Long Beach Arena.

Hoffman goes high to defend against No. 1 ranked University of San Francisco in AIA's first ever home game.

Runnin' Rebels presented a formidable opponent.

The Anaheim Convention Center crowd was even larger for this game. So was the final victory margin. The Runnin' Rebels never got their running game untracked, with AIA dominating the boards, 64 rebounds to 33, ("No rebound, no fastbreak," beamed Oates) and the scoring, 104-77.

One message was clear: AIA-USA was for real. The two big wins were giant steps for a team looking to establish itself as an amateur power worthy of representing the U.S.A. in the World Championships.

But the jury was still out. Indeed, AIA had proven it could beat the best college teams in the land. But beating the nation's best colleges and the world's best international teams are not synonymous feats. AIA needed to prove its case against a major international power before asking the Amateur Basketball Association of the United States (ABAUSA) to render a verdict on overseas opportunities. That test was to come sooner than anybody in AIA could imagine.

Another test, one that a player would have to face by himself, was even more imminent. This trial was far removed from the basketball court, and for Brad Hoffman, it was to be the ordeal of his young life.

NOTES

1. Dwight Chapin, "Twenty Years Later, USF is Back on Top," *Los Angeles Times*, Jan. 15, 1977, part III, p.4, col.3.
2. Skip Bayless, "The Mad, Mad Antics of USF Turn Coach Into a Basket Case," *Los Angeles Times*, March 25, 1977, part III, p.8, col. 1.
3. Ibid, p. 1, col.4.
4. John Hall, "So Help Me," *Los Angeles Times*, Jan. 17, 1977, part III, p.3.
5. Earl Gustkey, "USF is Handed First Loss But it Won't Count," *Los Angeles Times*, Jan. 21, 1977, part III, p. 1.
6. John Hall, "God Squadder," *Los Angeles Times*, Jan. 25, 1977 part III, p.3.
7. Sam Heys, "Upset," *Saturday Enquirer and Ledger* (Columbus, GA), Jan. 22, 1977, sports section, p. 1.

ROUGH TIMES AND RUSSIAN REFS

"A smooth sea never a skillful sailor made."

"Brad . . ." Becky Hoffman whispered urgently in her husband's ear. "Brad, wake up." She shook his shoulder, trying to rouse him.

It was 5:30 a.m. The couple, in a Sacramento, California hotel room, had journeyed to northern California with the team on its annual wives' trip. Becky had gone to bed early that night complaining of an aching stomach.

Abdominal pains are nothing out of the ordinary for a pregnant woman who expects to bear twins in two months. But the aches were more severe now — and coming intermittently. "Brad!" she said again, louder this time. Her husband finally rolled over; Becky told him what was happening.

"Honey, listen," he said as reassuringly as he could. "I know you don't feel good . . . the trip was hard on you. You're just tired. It's in your mind." Brad, unable to convince even himself, laid back down and acted like he was sleeping.

"It *can't* be the babies . . ." He didn't even want to form the thought. "They won't have a chance this much premature!"

By 8:30 a.m. the pains were more frequent and the couple's worst fears could no longer be denied. Brad got one of the team rental cars and hurried his wife to the hospital.

"Wait out here," the doctor commanded Brad upon arrival. Five minutes later attendants whisked Becky back out of the emergency room and down a corridor. Her 23-year-old husband ran to keep up with the cart, grasping her arm.

"We're rushing her up to surgery right now," an attendant hastily explained. "She's going to have the baby . . ." Hoffman slowed one of the doctors long enough to explain that Becky was expecting twins.

"I doubt if they'll weigh more than a pound-and-a-half each," the doctor replied. "I'm sorry, but I can't give them better than a 10% chance of survival."

Hoffman spent the next hour pleading with God. "Let them be all right," he prayed. The minutes dragged by.

When the doctor finally emerged the news was better than expected. "You've got two boys," he said. "One is two pounds, thirteen ounces, the other three pounds, two ounces. Your wife should recover without complications." Brad breathed more easily.

"The babies are breathing fine," the doctor added, "which is rare for infants of this size. But there's still a lot of danger; we'll have to keep them in intensive care for at least 10 days."

Mr. and Mrs. Charles L. Collings, parents of AIA staff member Dianna Collings, offered to put Brad up, and Becky too, when she got out of the hospital six days later. Brad reluctantly accepted. "I don't even know these people," he thought.

The team had to continue its schedule, but the players prayed daily for their teammate who stayed behind, his wife and their two infant sons, Nathanael and Benjamin.

Nathanael held his own, but on the 17th day

Benjamin suffered a massive brain hemorrhage. "His chances of surviving another night are one to 1,000," the doctors told the bewildered parents when they had rushed to the hospital.

"But we've prayed . . . and he was doing so good." Brad and Becky struggled that day, trying to come to grips with the grievous news. By evening they were able to go to the hospital chapel and pray together. "God, please don't take our baby," they pleaded. "We don't want you to take him." They prayed honestly, knowing that only God could spare their child. "Lord, it's out of our control. All we can do is ask that your will be done. We commit Benjamin to you."

The infant lived through the night and waged a stand-off battle with death for four days. "He's beaten the odds so far," the doctors acknowledged. "But there's still no way — you've got to accept it."

As the days passed there remained little visible reason for optimism. A tube running from his brain to his stomach helped reduce swelling by draining excess fluid, but gave the tiny infant a deathly appearance.

They often visited Benjamin together, as Becky records in the diary that she began keeping in mid-February: *"Brad and I both prayed today, silently laying our hands on him."* And later: *"He moved his left leg and right arm and yawned."* Any sign of life was encouraging.

Though it seemed illogical, Becky had a growing conviction that her baby was to be healed. She read in Mark chapter five how Jesus healed the ailing woman's hemorrhage. *"The Lord really spoke to me about Benjamin getting better,"* she wrote. Several days later Becky learned that Brad had come to the same conviction. To the doctors, however, the situation still seemed hopeless.

The team, meanwhile, was enjoying a fruitful

ministry and playing great basketball. It appeared
certain that AIA would sweep the games remaining on
its 1976-77 schedule. But that was before a certain
telephone call.

The call came first to an official of the Amateur
Basketball Association of the United States
(ABAUSA), in his Jacksonville, Ill. office. Yuri
Ozerov, assistant coach for the Soviet Red Army
basketball team, was calling from Moscow. Through
an interpreter, he was saying the Russians wanted
another game during their upcoming visit to the
United States.

"For crying out loud, Yuri, this is short notice,"
the U.S. official moaned. "Why couldn't we have set
this up weeks ago?"

The only reply was: "It is now possible."

Knowing of AIA's international aspirations, the
ABAUSA representative immediately called Dave
Hannah. It was now Hannah's turn to moan.

"Play the Russians six days from now?

That's impossible!" But even as he spoke Hannah
knew he must consider this offer. The opportunity to
play what was essentially Russia's national team might
not come again. "We'll get back to you," Hannah told
his caller.

"Make it soon," came the reply.

The AIA director quickly gathered some of his top
leadership. They didn't bother adjourning to a conference room, but instead stood in a circle in the
middle of the office lobby and prayed.

Staff members quickly contacted the Anaheim
Convention Center. It was booked, but the nearby
Long Beach Arena was available. A local company
would put a rush on ticket printing. Other staff visited
area newspapers and came away confident that the
game would generate plenty of coverage. "We can pull

it off, Lord willing," P.R. Director Hicks projected.

When Hannah returned the ABA call, only a few additional matters remained to be resolved. Some were financial details, but something else was of greater concern to the AIA director. The Russians were balking at AIA's traditional halftime presentation. Hannah, refusing to compromise, made his position clear: "No halftime presentation, no game."

The matter was resolved and the game was on. The Campus Crusade athletic staff had toiled weeks to sell less than 7,000 tickets for each of the first two home games. Now they had just five days to sell 10,000 tickets for the Russian game and worked almost around the clock to do so.

When Oates returned with the team from a short trip to Canada he had good news awaiting him. Brad Hoffman would play against the Russians. "Getting away for a few days might be the best thing for you," one of the doctors in Sacramento had advised the team leader.

When the word got out about the game, tickets began to sell like hot shares on the commodity market. Weary but excited AIA staff watched an astounding crowd of 10,239 file through the gates at the Long Beach Arena. One Jewish sports editor was equally amazed by the crowd. "You people haven't converted me yet," he said, "but what you did in five days was like God parting the Red Sea!"

"It was an intensely played game — even violent at times," observed Earl Gustkey of the *Los Angeles Times*. The lead changed hands 15 times before it ended.

AIA's big men, Forrest and Drollinger, weren't around at the end. Forrest took an elbow to the stomach from the Soviet's giant 7-foot-5 center, Vladimir Tkachenko. The blow sent his heart into an irregular beat. Medics carried him out of the arena on a stretcher and rushed him to nearby St. Mary's Medical Center. There he was examined, released and told: "Stay out of the game." Drollinger fouled out with 8:56 remaining. But it would have taken more than the AIA big men to alter this game's finish.

Mel Ross and Michael Davidov were the game officials, Ross of the NCAA's Pac-8 conference and Davidov reputedly the Soviet Union's No.1 referee. As Gustkey wrote, "until the final 10 seconds, there was little cause to question Davidov's work."

With the Soviets nursing a 108-105 lead he called a midcourt traveling violation on Hoffman after an inbounds pass. Ten thousand plus fans leaped howling to their feet. The whistle had clearly sounded before Hoffman touched the ball!

The little guard slammed the ball hard on the court and yanked his head around to look at Davidov in disbelief. "What!" He stomped toward the referee in a rage. "What did you call? I didn't even touch the ball!" Hoffman was screaming, his body heaving with anger, but he was still barely heard over the din of the raving crowd.

It was more than an unfair call that evoked Hoffman's outburst. The burdens on a young man with two sons fighting for life, a depressed wife and medical bills approaching the $50,000 mark had taken their toll. But the referee ignored Hoffman who eventually walked away, demoralized.

One second after Davidov's call, Ross called a charge against a Soviet player and the boos turned to cheers. But Davidov, not to be upstaged, reversed the call and allowed the Russians to retain possession. Popcorn boxes and hotdog wrappers rained down on the court; for a moment, the crowd threatened to erupt violently.

The Soviet official's decision held and time ran out for AIA with Eldon Lawyer at the foul line trying to bounce his second shot off the rim for a tip-in. It didn't work.

AIA had nevertheless made a good showing against the Soviets in the 108-106 loss. The performance certainly had not hurt the team's chances of going to the World Championships — perhaps the showing even enhanced it.

One would never have guessed this, however, from a visit to the AIA locker room. Losing was a bitter pill to swallow for the team whose 26-game winning streak had been snapped with a bitter and highly controversial defeat.

A mournful silence enveloped the room. The only sound came from the corner where an exhausted Brad Hoffman sat, head in hands, weeping.

CHAPTER
TEN

PROVEN CHARACTER

". . . knowing that the testing of your faith produces endurance. And let endurance have its perfect result, that you may be perfect and complete, lacking in nothing."

James 1:3,4

The Soviets were at the top of Oates' priority list when it came time to arrange the team's 1977-78 schedule. A date was soon set — the Russians would return for a season-opening rematch on November 2, 1977.

But the Soviet rivalry did not occupy Brad Hoffman's mind in the meantime. Immediately after the first game against the Russians he hurried to Sacramento. His first stop was the hospital where he found his boys still holding their own.

After a few days, in fact, Nathanael came home. This was a welcomed development, but nonetheless an additional strain on Brad and Becky. Now they rarely saw each other: one of them invariably stayed at the hospital with Benjamin while the other took care of Nate.

The people of Elk Grove Baptist Church, most of whom did not know the Hoffmans, hosted a baby shower. The couple received a crib, playpen, bathtub, hamper and some clothing. *"The Lord has been so good."* wrote a thankful Becky in her diary.

A series of minor operations would be necessary for Benjamin, but the doctors, now optimistic, believed he might join his brother at home before long.

One Sunday, Mom and Dad brought Nate to see Benjamin. They took pictures of the twins together. By Easter, Benji, as the nurses had begun calling him, weighed five pounds, thirteen ounces. Becky wrote, *"We are so thankful for him."*

The renewed hopes for Benji's recovery made it that much harder when the doctors came on April 12, after another routine surgery, to tell Brad his son had died. "We were closing up the incision and his heart just stopped . . ."

Brad felt like his own heart had stopped. He fell against the wall and slid nearly to the floor. Some of the medical team stood there trying to comfort him. "We just don't know what happened . . ." they kept saying.

Becky and the Collings had gathered in another room to await word of the surgery. When Brad came to tell them, they wept together for a long time.

Driving home that night Hoffman had a flat tire. As he worked to change it, he became increasingly angry with God. "Why did you take him?" He did not speak the question, but nevertheless wanted an answer. "I thought You were going to let him live. He was getting better!" This marked the beginning of a bitterness that nearly destroyed him and Becky.

"I quit praying and going to church. My whole relationship with God was broken," Brad said. "Then I began to seclude myself, which hurt my relationship with Becky and everybody else.

"I'm quitting the team," he told Oates. Hoffman accepted a job in North Carolina, even though he and Becky had no peace of mind about leaving AIA.

Losing its floor leader was a severe blow to the

team's chances of going to the world championships. AIA had already suffered another big loss: Bayard Forrest had decided to sign with the NBA's Phoenix Suns, believing that to be God's will for him.

Oates tried to reason with the distraught Hoffman. "Brad, listen to me. You can't go on being bitter toward God. It's only hurting you."

Only after Hoffman agreed to attend Campus Crusade's annual staff training that summer in Colorado did he begin to overcome his bitterness. Brad spent a number of hours there talking with a staff member who also had suffered the loss of a child. "He told me that until I was willing to thank God for what happened, my relationship with the Lord would not be right, nor with Becky, or Nate or anybody," Hoffman said. "I told him 'I can't thank God for that . . .'"

"Then he read I Thessalonians 5:18 where it says to give thanks in everything. 'You don't have to be thankful for the circumstances and the way it turned out,' he told me, 'but be thankful that God is in control.'

"I went back to my room a couple of nights later, gritted my teeth and said it. Then I thanked God every night for awhile because I didn't know if I meant it at first. God started working in my life at that point, and I began to get back in fellowship with Him."

Ironically, Becky's bitterness first surfaced at this time. Home and alone for the first time since Benjamin's death, she now felt the impact.

"At first," Becky recalls, "it was like a story — it really hadn't happened to us. But when Brad was at staff training and I was by myself with Nate and I had to take care of him by myself, in a new place . . . I didn't know my neighbors, I felt all alone, all the AIA people were gone, we weren't in a church . . . that's when I started growing really bitter and depressed. I didn't care about taking care of Nate, about cleaning the house, or doing anything — not even to get dressed. I just didn't care."

The compassionate care of another staff wife helped Becky deal with her depression. "Kathy Phipps talked me into joining an Old Testament Bible study fellowship," Becky said, "and she got a baby sitter for me. There were lots of times I wouldn't go, but she kept encouraging me to, so most of the time I did.

"But I wanted to know if all the things I grew up learning were true. I would catch myself saying a prayer because I was in the habit of doing it; then I would say 'I'm not going to do that . . . He's not really there . . . He's not real . . .' So I was going to this Bible study feeling like that."

A number of weeks later, after Brad returned, Becky was doing a Bible study on David from the book of Samuel. "Saul was chasing him," she said. "He was fleeing for his life, and I started feeling sorry for David. I asked God, 'Why did you do this to him — he never did anything to you? You're the one who said he was going to be king and yet he's fleeing for his life.' "

As Becky continued reading, however, she began to recognize God's many provisions for David — the guidance of Samuel the priest, the precious friendship of Jonathan, 400 loyal followers — all during this time of greatest need.

Becky realized something. "Things started coming back to me," she said. "I started making a list of all the things God had provided for us: the hospital in Sacramento is the second largest and one of the best in California for delivering babies. And the Collings' were so good to us. They took us in like their own children and Mr. Collings headed up the effort, along with the Aid Association for Lutherans, that raised

$50,000 to cover our bills. And because of all the time we spent in the hospital, I had a chance to talk to many of the nurses about Christ."

Some anger, however, still lingered. Another lesson from Scripture was needed to complete Becky's healing.

"I was reading the Scripture about how God's Son died for us," she said. "I thought, well . . . my son died too. So big deal, why is it so much more important that your Son died?

"But then I read on . . . it said that God gave *His* Son willingly. We did everything in our power to keep ours. But God chose to give Jesus for us who were unworthy. That hit me hard. Plus, we still had Nate. God gave His *only* Son."

"I wouldn't have given my son for anyone," her husband acknowledges. "But now I understand better what it meant for God to give His Son for me."

The Hoffmans rejoined the team. Brad knew he belonged with AIA. His goal of seeing his life count for Christ could not, for now, be better realized elsewhere. And the Russians still stood between him and another goal: AIA's shot at a world championship.

The U.S.A.'s representative for the next FIBA World Basketball Championships, to be held in Manila in September of 1978, would be chosen at the conclusion of the approaching season (the French-named "Federation Internationale de Basketball Amateur" sponsors the tournament every two years). This made AIA's 1977-78 slate more crucial than any. And the toughest.

The Russians showed up with their full National Team for "Borscht vs. apple pie," round two. It was a stronger team, with one notable exception — referee Michael Davidov stayed home.

But the Soviets had more on their "to do in

America" list than just "beat AIA." In fact, upon arrival they were more interested in the whereabouts of a Penney's store than a practice facility. All of them came armed with shopping lists to put any "bourgeois westerner" to shame. Priority items included records, stereos, Levi jeans and Mickey Mouse shirts.

"Some of them had 8½ x 11 lists of records they wanted," said Phil Palady, a member of the AIA wrestling team who served as an escort during the Russian visit. The wrestler watched incredulously as *each* of the Russians bought more than $1,000 worth of records.

Soviet citizens have, of course, been warned that these examples of "imperialistic decadence" are harmful to the "health of the proletariat." But the records also bring top ruble on the black market. And Soviet officials tend to look the other way when "capitalistic" items are carried into the motherland by their athletic heroes.

One Soviet player asked Palady to drive him to Montgomery Ward; he wanted to look at "fancy telephones — like you might have in your bedroom if you were rich." The athlete bought three at $51 each. "Two are for gifts," he said.

As Phil and the player were driving back, the AIA athlete found that, if he talked slowly, he could communicate with the Russian. They talked about Christ and His love. The player was responsive and listened intently to Palady. "One of my relatives is a Christian," the Russian said. "She has tried many times to make me believe." He then told Palady, "If you had tried to talk to any of the other players about God they would have laughed at you."

Soviet Coach Alexandr Gomelsky was less responsive. When asked what he thought about AIA's spiritual goals he said, "They're a team that's out to advertise, to propagate a cause, propaganda . . ."

No, Alexandr, Coach Oates and his players might have said, this team takes its evangelism *and* its basketball seriously. Indeed, the Soviet coach found out soon enough. With AIA's flashy new forward Alonzo Bradley hitting often from the corner (23 points), AIA dominated the battle throughout and won, 93-84. Two American referees worked the game which was void of controversy. Oates and Hannah knew that the ABAUSA took note of the key win. An ABAUSA official, in fact, commented that "if AIA can keep its team together they should at least be considered for the world championships."

But keeping the team together proved difficult. Alonzo Bradley, after leading the squad to 18 straight wins to open the season, received a $300,000 Christmas gift in the form of a contract from the NBA Houston Rockets. Oates was flabbergasted when Bradley called to say he was leaving the team.

"Alonzo, you made a commitment," the coach told him. But the decision was made. Bradley left the team in the lurch. And yet, the player's thinking was not hard to understand. The youngest of 16 children, Alonzo wanted to give financial aid to his widowed mother, a welfare recipient.

With Bradley's departure, Irv Kiffin moved back into the starting position that his temporary teammate had taken from him. "Kiff" admits that he struggled with a bad attitude during his bench-riding interim. "I felt like I wasn't being treated right," he remembers. But just before Bradley left, Kiffin came to grips with the problem. "I realized, if I'm playing for God it doesn't make any difference if I start. It's only important that I do my best. It was my pride that caused my bad attitude."

AIA continued its winning ways with Kiffin back

in his old spot. Only UCLA's incredible streak of 88 consecutive wins at the time ranked ahead of AIA's 35 straight against colleges (over two seasons).

Hannah noted that people had a different attitude about the team. "I went up for a game against Fresno State a few years ago," he said. "We weren't too good then and they beat us by 25 points. I heard people saying, 'What do you expect? — they're Christians.' But this year our program had developed and we went up and beat them by 25. This time people were saying, 'What do you expect? — they're professionals'! "

Ironically, a few people now complained to Hannah that AIA was emphasizing winning *too* much. "Actually, we're committed to losing," Hannah assured them with tongue-in-cheek. "We've just been unlucky lately."

But even the thrill of winning could not compare to the excitement of seeing God work in an individual's life. Ralph Drollinger will never forget one woman he sat next to on an airplane. She had been pre-boarded in a wheel chair and was suffering from an advanced case of throat cancer.

The woman and her husband were flying from Fort Lauderdale, Florida to a hospital in Virginia, where she would have a throat operation. The middle-aged woman was obviously suffering as she repeatedly coughed up mucus into a tissue.

Though it was early in the morning and the team had played a game the night before, Ralph chose not to rest, but showed his concern and listened as the husband and wife told their story. He then talked with them about Christ.

"Sometimes God allows struggles to bring people to His Son," he told them. His listeners had never heard of a personal relationship with Jesus Christ. When Ralph shared the Four Spiritual Laws booklet with them, both trusted Christ as Savior.

After returning to southern California, Ralph got a letter from the couple. Doctors at the Virginia hospital had reported the cancer mysteriously gone. Drollinger rejoiced; not only had two people come to Christ, but one had been healed as well. And it had nothing to do with Ralph's basketball prowess, only his availability to God.

The team continued to roar along the way to a near-perfect 32-2 record. AIA's chances for the world championships looked good — unless the ABAUSA demanded perfection.

But now the NBA came courting a third AIA candidate. And, according to a March 8 speculative story in the *Los Angeles Herald Examiner,* Ralph Drollinger would become the third AIA player in a year to take his plum from the pros. "The former UCLA center is being pursued by the New Jersey Nets," wrote Mitch Chortkoff. The *Orange County Register* also reported that New Jersey was "close to signing" Drollinger to a "six-figure, multi-year" contract and quoted a Net official as saying Drollinger would be offered "a contract he can't refuse."

A portion of the reports were proven true; the Nets officially offered a three-year $400,000 no-cut package. Some sources said New Jersey would negotiate into the million-dollar range, but those reports were never confirmed.

At any rate, two things were clear: the offer was a far cry from the $7,500 yearly missionary scholarship Drollinger was getting from AIA, and the team could forget the world championships if he went pro.

Intense defense: Tim Hall gave his all in World Championship game with Yugoslavia (Brad Hoffman in background).

Drollinger explains why he refused offer the pros said he couldn't.

Hoffman addresses audience at halftime: "Now I understand more of what it meant for God to give up His Son for me."

CHAPTER ELEVEN

PLAY RICH OR PREACH POOR?

". . . money talks, nobody walks."

Brian Zevnik
New York Tribune,
writing about Ralph Drollinger

During his days as a high school superstar near San Diego, California, Ralph Drollinger's ambition was to be a millionaire.

"I equated success with money," Ralph recalls. "I had seen a lot of nice homes and had a file of ideas for designing my own house. I wanted one with a firemen's pole from the top floor to the ground floor," he chuckles.

Money was a big factor in Drollinger's decision to attend UCLA. "Their pro prospects," he figured, "sign for at least $10,000 more than guys out of other schools."

But a lot had happened in the life of Ralph Kim Drollinger between Grossmont High and the UCLA pedigree he picked up on his way to the NBA. He'd grown another few inches and become less shy; but the biggest changes became evident after he received Jesus Christ as His Savior.

As a Christian, Ralph learned to deal with his tendencies toward moodiness and saw dramatic changes in his attitudes and priorities. A primary

example: serving God became more important than
making money.

Ralph's changed perspective did not make the
decision he now faced any easier, however. He flew to
New York City where he planned to make his
announcement at a press conference. Oates sent
Gratzke with him, figuring that his lofty center could
use some extra prodding to stay in shape while in the
city. After all, AIA still had to face a talented contingent of collegiate all-stars in the first Coaches All-
American Game and represent the United States in an
important South American basketball tournament.

Ralph's first day in the big city had a unique
emotional impact on him. "There were hordes of
people on the subways," he recalls. "It was a sea of
faces — thousands of them — and many looked so
empty. A lot of the people were reading newspapers,
and it occurred to me that the next day many of them
would be reading about what Jesus Christ means to
me."

At the crowded press conference, Drollinger asked
his hushed audience a rhetorical question: "Where can
I best invest my life to tell others about the love and
forgiveness of Jesus Christ? . . . When one holds this
as his primary motive in making decisions, the factor
of money greatly diminishes.

"God has given me an exciting ministry with
Athletes in Action. Does He want me to walk away
from that ministry? I think not."

Drollinger explained two personal goals: first, to
introduce sports fans to Jesus Christ and, second, to
encourage fellow followers of Christ to invest their
lives (even if that means sacrificing money) in
spreading the love of Christ. He said he would remain
with Athletes in Action until at least 1980 before
reconsidering pro ball.

Drollinger finished by quoting missionary Jim Elliot, who sacrificed his life to reach a primitive South American tribe with the gospel: " 'He is no fool who gives up what he cannot keep, to gain what he cannot lose.' "

The media response was overwhelming. All three networks — ABC, CBS and NBC — ran footage of the conference or excerpts from the statement on evening news shows across the country. Radio stations nationwide played the story as a sports lead throughout the day. United Press International ran a national wire story; AP carried three separate stories.

Wrote Brian Zevnik of the *New York Tribune,* ". . . Ralph Drollinger saddened the hearts of New Jersey Net fans, dealt a blow to the rebuilding efforts of the . . . NBA team, and refuted the all-prevalent philosophy in sports today: money talks, nobody walks. Drollinger is cut from different cloth."[1]

Steve Bisheff, writing for Ralph's hometown *San Diego Union,* later wrote: "In this era of the spoiled, affluent, self-centered professional athlete, Ralph Drollinger did an amazing thing the other day. He chose his own deep-seated beliefs over a huge stack of thousand-dollar bills. He picked his personal commitment over a shiny, new car and a wardrobe full of flashy clothes.

". . . this move by Drollinger is more spectacular than any he ever made at UCLA. With one simple 'No' he reached more people than he ever would averaging 20 points in the National Basketball Association."[2]

Mickey Charles, who writes a sports betting column, added: "When Ralph Drollinger, a 7-foot-2 former UCLA center turns down a $400,000 three-year, no-cut contract from the New Jersey Nets to stay with a crusading basketball team, Athletes in Action, that's dedication . . . I'm sure you find it strange to see admiration of this kind being expressed by someone who spends his time handicapping and analyzing sports. What I do is easy. Ralph Drollinger receives a $7,500 missionary scholarship from Campus Crusade for Christ."[3]

Those who know Ralph well weren't as surprised as the reporters. John Wooden, his coach at UCLA, said, "I wasn't surprised in any way, knowing the way he thinks about things. But maybe this could be a revelation to people, inasmuch as we read about players wanting to renegotiate contracts they've made in good faith, wanting more and more and more." Speaking at a banquet, Wooden referred to the intangible, spiritual benefits of playing with AIA and said, "Ralph got a better deal."

Drollinger rejoined his teammates in California for AIA's season-ending contest against a powerful contingent of 10 All-Americans that included the nation's leading scorer, Freeman Williams, UCLA's Raymond Townsend and Arkansas' Marvin Delph. While all-star coach Digger Phelps poor-mouthed his chances at a pregame press conference, claiming, "Athletes in Action has one of the best franchises in the NBA," his own All-American arsenal was impressive. The combined averages of the 10 came to 195.4 points per game. "We're hoping to hold them under their average," Oates said.

His hopes were realized. AIA polished off the all-stars, 103-88. But there was little time to savor the victory. The players hurried home for about four hours sleep. They had to catch an important flight in the morning. The ABAUSA had decided to test AIA's mettle in international competition by sending the team to the Christopher Columbus Cup Western Hemisphere Championships in Argentina. It was a grueling test. Consider the trip itself:

— The players flew to Guatemala City, arriving late in the afternoon. After a three-hour lay-over during which the plane was searched for a bomb, they continued on to Caracas, Venezuela, landing at 4 p.m.

— From Caracas the players flew to Buenos Aires, Argentina, arriving 24 hours after leaving California. There the team boarded a bus and was led through the city at recklessly high speeds by two policemen in a 1964 Falcon. The driver ran any car that crossed his path off the road, sometimes ramming the Falcon into the side of another car, while his partner shouted threats and waved a shotgun out the window.

— The team was taken to a missionary school and fed "meat pies stuffed with spinach," by one player's description, and given mats to lie on.

— The players were soon awakened and flown 600 miles to Resistencia in northern Argentina, arriving at the hotel at 5:30 p.m. There, the U.S.A. contingent was met by their smiling host, Jorge, who had his own welcoming committee waiting — "friendly" girls and lots of booze.

"Jorge was a real character," broadcaster Iverson remembers. "He was expecting some American swinger-types. He couldn't understand why we weren't interested in his hospitality."

The team did not play until 11:00 that night but officials wanted them at the arena at 7:00 for the opening ceremonies. Later, they beat Uruguay, 104-88. After the game the players were obligated to attend a rollicking post-game dinner party ("Oh boy," they groaned.) and finally collapsed into bed between 3 and 4 a.m.

The next day, most of the players slept 12-14 hours, so it was not surprising when they played sluggishly against Puerto Rico and lost, 88-76.

The loss put the team in an unenviable position.

AIA had to beat Brazil by at least 22 points to advance
to the final round. Hall and Drollinger held a prayer
meeting the day of the game. "Our goal is to be the top
amateur team in the world," one player reminded the
gathering, "and we're not going to kid anybody if we
don't win here."

"Everybody was praying, seeking the Lord, getting
right," Hall remembers.

Iverson sensed "an electricity in the air."

It seemed that half of the Resistencia population
had turned out to cheer *against* the Americans. AIA
suffered the consequences of a bad first impression
with the local basketball fanatics. On opening night,
they had trotted casually onto the court for warm-ups,
as always. But South Americans are accustomed to
players entering with great fanfare — shouting and
waving to the crowd. So, "hotdogging" in North
America is traditional courtesy in South America.

"The fans thought we were aloof, and they never
let us forget it," Hoffman said. Actually, Hoffman was
the lone American to win the hearts of the crowd. They
labeled him the "Little White Seal from Antarctica"
because he "clapped so much."

Seven thousand people packed into the arena for
the AIA-Brazil game. The arena was not built to hold
more than 5,000, and yet, another 1,200 leaned
against the wire fence that served as the structure's
walls. The throng made a frightful racket, chanting
"Bra-Zeel! Bra-zeel! Bra-zeel!" — to no avail. In
perhaps the best complete game in its history, AIA led
by 10 at the end of the first half and poured it on in the
second to win by 26 points — 116-90.

The next game, a 95-89 win over Canada, coupled
with two Puerto Rico losses, sent AIA into the finals
where Drollinger dominated the boards (17 rebounds)
and AIA dominated Argentina, 81-69, for the cham-

pionship of the Western Hemisphere.

All things considered, it was a courageous performance by Athletes in Action. The team had passed the ABAUSA's mid-term exam with high marks. "AIA is a credit to the United States and basketball for playing so well under adverse conditions," said ABAUSA president George Killian. "We are looking forward to having AIA represent the United States in basketball in the future." Translation: "AIA has the inside track to represent the United States at the World Championships in Manila."

The U.S.A. *needed* a good World Championships representative. The United States had last won the tournament in 1954. Even for a tournament held every four years, that indicates a lot of failure. Part of the problem was that the United States doesn't take the tournament seriously enough. "The FIBA championship, to the World, is the No. 1 basketball event," said an ABAUSA official. "But in the United States it has been a nonentity. This is bigger than the Olympics to international basketball people."

Why hasn't the country that gave birth to basketball paid more attention to the sport's World Championship? Dave Hannah says: "The only international event we Americans take seriously is the Olympics. We're becoming more of a one-world community every day, but athletically-speaking, America still has its head in the sand."

Typically, America throws together a group of college players for the World Championships that don't have time to gel as a team. AIA had argued all along — "Why not send a proven *team* to the Championships to give the needed cohesiveness?"

And the athletic ministry didn't hide another motive for wanting to go to the World Championships. While a FIBA championship would do little to enhance AIA's platform in the United States, it could open great doors overseas. As Coach Oates said, "We're interested in winning these games not for the glory that it will bring to us, but for the glory that it will bring to Jesus Christ — and the opportunities it will provide for us to share His love throughout the world."

The long-awaited invitation did come. And now, the "God Squad" hoped to win the World Championships for America after a 24-year drought.

Nobody thought it would be easy, but neither did anyone imagine it would prove as tough as it did.

CHAPTER
TWELVE

BRING ON THE WORLD

"This is a three-year dream come true."

Dave Hannah

If the Western Hemisphere Championships taught the AIA players how to deal with adversity, the World Championships would teach them how to deal with calamity. That much became evident before the team even began training camp.

After a summer of youth camps, clinics and speaking engagements, the team assembled in August to find it had no place to practice. The usual facilities — the Salvation Army gym in Santa Ana and The East Bluff Boys Club in Newport Beach — were unavailable, but not ideal anyway: both had courts eight feet too short.

"We've contacted 35 or 40 different colleges, high schools, everything," Hannah told a reporter, "and they're either refinishing their floors or tied up with summer programs."

When the team finally did locate a practice gym, AIA's hopes for a world championship suffered another setback. Ralph Drollinger injured his knee. Immediate surgery was required — he looked doubtful for the Championships, as did AIA's chances of winning.

Minus its dominating center, the team took off for a pre-tournament tour of Australia. After two weeks of hopping around the kangaroo country, the players found themselves more "wornout" than "warmed-up." "It was foolishness," Tim Hall said, "for us to go over there, run all over the country for two weeks and have our energy sapped."

Why did they go? Ironically, the world's richest country lacked adequate funds to send its representative to Asia, but the Aussies had plenty and offered some of it for the privilege of tuning up against the Americans.

More bad news awaited the U.S.A. team in Manila. Larry Johnson, a 6-foot-3 guard from Kentucky and one of two players added to complete the American roster, was sent home because he was said to have lost his amateur status, having participated in several pre-season NBA games. AIA's Dave Iverson attended the press briefing where the Johnson case was discussed.

"An amateur basketball player," FIBA Secretary General Boris Stankovich of Yugoslavia explained, "is someone who dedicates himself to this sport because he likes and loves it."

Iverson's hand shot up. "Does this mean that Kareem Abdul Jabbar doesn't like basketball?" he asked.

"Oh no," Stankovich answered. "It's the intent with which he plays. It depends on what he's going to do with the money."

"What do you mean?" Iverson, puzzled by the answer, asked.

"An amateur is going to use the money to better himself," Stankovich said.

Even more puzzled, the AIA representative said, "Are you trying to tell me that Jabbar is not going to use the money to better himself?" Iverson was persistent, though he knew his argument was in vain.

"Dumb American," officials from several countries were heard muttering.

"You just don't understand," other officials kept telling him. A *lot* of Americans don't understand how a European can be paid $100,000 a year, receive free use of a house and car, and, with a straight face, still call himself an "amateur." Or how a 20-year-old Russian can be appointed a major in the Red Army when his only military responsibility is to win amateur basketball "battles."

"You're right," Iverson said, "I just don't understand."

The FIBA definition, in essence, said an amateur can be paid to play basketball anywhere in the world *except* in the National Basketball Association of the United States.

If the air seemed thick at the FIBA meeting . . . it was. The Philippines are bathed in sweltering heat, and 95% humidity makes the air heavy and movement slow. Even the sleeveless nets the players called practice shirts seemed too heavy. Hoping to help his players adjust to the sticky conditions, Oates decreed that no air conditioners be used in hotel rooms or on team buses.

But stuffy rooms and buses were only one form of inconvenience the players endured. Women sometimes made advances on hotel elevators and via telephone.

Outside on the street, hawkers were even less discreet, shouting, "Pretty girl, pretty girl," to entice passers-by. But when the players talked about Christ instead of price, the propositions quickly ended. One "overture," however, was humorous.

Oates, Gratzke and Iverson were riding in a cab whose driver, in a vulgar manner, persisted in trying to interest them in some prostitutes. Oates and "Iver" could not help but chuckle when Gratzke, making sure he didn't offend the cabbie, said, "No, we're Christians, but thanks for thinking of us."

Not everyone was out to hustle the Americans. Most of the locals, in fact, expressed their hopes for a U.S.A. win in the championships. From waitresses in restaurants, to hotel employees, the sentiment was consistent, "We hope you win."

At practice, the day before the first game, the players were amazed when Ralph Drollinger showed up in the gym. He was supposed to be in a hospital bed or at least at home recovering, but here he was, moving up and down the court on what appeared to be a strong knee.

The big guy's return gave the team a needed boost, but Oates was still nervous about AIA's first opponent, Australia . . . Australia?! Wasn't this the team AIA had whipped seven times during the early tour? It was, and Oates knew the Aussies were familiar with every move in his team's repertoire. "We're just due to lose to these guys," he feared.

Were it not for a strong performance by back-up center Ernest Wansley, AIA might have done just that. As it was, the Americans avoided an embarrassing upset, squeaking by the Australians, 77-75.

After viewing the Yankee opener, Zoran Slavnic of Yugoslavia boasted to an American journalist, "If we go on the standard of today, we can easily beat them by 30 points."

In game two, however, the U.S.A. got its offensive act together and blitzed an undermanned Dominican Republic team, 104-49.

Only the most diehard fans showed up for AIA's third game against the tough Czechoslovakian national team. The players barely made it themselves: the team buses had to find their way through darkened and rain-swollen streets after a ferocious monsoon dumped a foot of rain and knocked out lights in the city.

The raging storm outside compensated for the absence of crowd noise inside as AIA pulled away from the Czechs in the final nine minutes to post an impressive 96-79 win. The victory put AIA in the semi-final rounds; the coveted world championship was in reach.

After the Czech win, the team enjoyed three days off. On the first day Tim Hall sat in a hotel breezeway when he heard a young voice say, "Hey, Joe." Hall turned to find a Filipino boy standing beside him.

"How ya doing?" Hall said, smiling big. They began talking — mostly about basketball and why people in America are so tall. At one point the conversation turned to Christ, and before long there were 12 enthralled boys surrounding the American. Hall explained how they could know God personally. Several of them invited Christ into their lives.

"Tell you what," Tim said when he had to leave. "I'll be here tomorrow at the same time. You be here, too."

Hall brought Drollinger and Kiffin with him the next day. The boys had spread the news to their buddies and 25 of them showed up! The athletes divided the youngsters into three groups: The first consisted of new boys who had not yet heard the gospel; a second group learned how they could have assurance of their salvation; a third learned some basic biblical promises. Word spread further by day three — 35 youngsters crowded into the breezeway to learn about God's love.

One night the players and coaches were special guests at an executive banquet sponsored by Campus Crusade. Those attending the dinner chuckled at the

sight of 5-foot-8 Coach Oates standing on the
speakers's platform beside 7-foot-2 Drollinger. Joked
Oates, "As you can see, Ralph and I don't see eye to
eye on anything."

Between banquets, practices and speaking engagements,the players had little time left for sightseeing.
But two veterans at covering AIA basketball — photo-
grapher Tom Mills and AIA Magazine Editor Bill
Horlacher — found time for a guided raft trip under a
cascading waterfull. Both thought they recognized the
third tourist who stepped onto their raft.

"Isn't that . . . ?" Mills said, trying to recollect the
name.

"It sure is," Horlacher said. "Our old buddy
Michael Davidov." The Russian ref turned out to be
an amiable fellow. Davidov had time for sightseeing,
but some of his comrades were apparently quite busy
at the championships. A western referee told Iverson
that a Russian had stopped by his room one day with a
suitcase full of gifts — "compliments of the Soviet
delegation."

"Such a nice guy, " Iverson joked. Iverson and the
western referee had become friends during the
Christopher Columbus Cup and were talking over
lunch in a hotel dining room. The referee, who later
that day would officiate the USSR-Yugoslavia game,
had also been designated as an official for the championship game to be played the following Saturday. "I
was happy just to get out of my room today," he told
Iverson.

"Any special reason?" Iverson asked.

"Yeah, the Russians won't leave me alone. Today
they want me at their reception. And they've already
chosen to 'honor' me next Saturday morning as one of
the top three officials of the tournament!"

The Russians were no doubt planning to play in

Saturday's championship game, but so were the other leading contenders, including AIA. AIA's plan, however, suffered a jolt in game four against Italy. By game's end three Yanks had fouled out, several others carried four personals and AIA stood on the short end of an 81-80 score. The upset loss was a blow to the team's championship hopes, and yet, it was not uncommon for the eventual champion to lose one contest during the tournament. "We've been down worse than this before," Hoffman reminded his teammates.

The next opponent, though, was Yugoslavia, one of the favorites in the tournament, and conquerors of Italy by 32 points. Oates said of the Yugoslavians, "They do things mechanically, like they've done them a million times. Yet," he added, "we have freedom in playing for Christ, and we don't have to worry about the results. I think you'll see a team that will give a tremendous effort tonight."

He was right. AIA played its finest game of the tournament and led in the second half. But again fouls hurt badly: the Yanks went to the foul line only seven times to the eastern Europeans' 24.

Though the referees, it seemed, took a stricter interpretation of the American habit of "hand-checking" on defense, there was no reason to suspect bias in the officiating.

The Americans scored five more baskets than the eastern Europeans, but it wasn't enough. As the buzzer sounded, the scoreboard lights flashed the death knell of a four-year dream: Yugoslavia 100, USA 93. The tournament continued but AIA knew its championship hopes were essentially ended.

After a close win over Canada and a two-point loss to Brazil, the team endured humiliation at the hands of the Soviet Union. The Russians dealt the Christians a

97-76 thrashing that evened AIA's record at a mediocre
4-4. Doing much of the damage was the Soviets'
answer to "Lurch" of the Adams Family — 7-foot-5,
280 lb., Vladimir Tkachenko. One journalist was
amazed at how smooth the giant played: "He can do
more than just stand there and grunt."

AIA managed to win its final two contests, beating
the Philippines, and for a second time, Canada, to
finish 6-4 and fifth in the 14-team field. Yugoslavia
was the eventual champion, stopping the defending
champion Russians 81-80 in the final.

Among those who observed the American demise
at the World Championships was Dale Brown, L.S.U.
basketball coach. Brown later told a reporter, "I wish
you could have been with me as I walked the streets of
Manila. People were shocked that we were losing.
They hate Communism with a passion.

"The Russians use (victories) to brainwash people
that the United States is weak, that Communism is
better. We are so dumb that we don't know we lose
great prestige around the world when the Russians
beat us."[1]

Failure. It was hard to accept—even hard to
believe — for a team that had come so far toward its
ambitious goal. Was this the same team that only
months before had finished 37-4 and won the western
hemisphere championship? It hardly seemed possible.
What went wrong?

Certainly the draining tour of Australia was a
factor. And the American "hand-checking" habit was
costly at the free throw line, as was perhaps AIA's lack
of a zone defense. The team lacked depth at center
because Drollinger, out of shape after his lay-off, could
be used only sparingly. Another factor, though less
easily defined, was nonetheless real. Iverson may have
said it best: "They were tight, not relaxed enough. The

mission got in the way of their ability to enjoy the trip."

Whatever the reasons, the players felt they played below their potential. None of them made excuses. "We deserved to get beat," said Tim Hall, "and we got beat."

Drollinger looked at the FIBA debacle from a faith perspective. "You learn about the sovereignty of God," he said. "He is still in control even though we lost. I don't think God is as concerned about our winning or losing as He is about how our hearts are toward Him."

The World Championship disappointment reminded Hannah of an important principle. "We can never lose sight of the fact," he said, "that our power lies not in our ability to win basketball games, but in the power of the gospel of Jesus Christ."

But failing at what seemed like the greatest opportunity in the team's history was still hard to come to grips with. "We couldn't help but wonder, 'Why Lord?' " Hall said. "When it looked like we could win the World Championships and have a great platform for You, why haven't things worked out?' "

Hall answered his own question. "The first thing we can learn is that God doesn't withhold any good thing, that all things work together for good and that we need to be thankful for this. Our team's going to take this as an opportunity for education."

Education indeed. AIA returned to the States to teach a "how-to-play basketball" course at some of America's top universities. The learners included Marquette, Arkansas, Ohio State, Alabama and Nevada-Las Vegas, all of whom tasted defeat at the hands of the Christian team.

But the course in international athletics that AIA received at the World Championships would prove invaluable in the years ahead. In Manila the team saw first hand the far-reaching impact and significance that athletics has worldwide. They began to understand what Communist nations perceived long ago — one fruit of athletic victory is influence. In a world where the battle is for men's minds, the results go far beyond the scoreboard. Every American should know how far beyond.

FOOTNOTES

1. Dale Brown, "At Least One Coach Believes Olympic Boycott Is a Blessing," *Los Angeles Times*, June 6, 1980, Part III, p. 2, col. 1.

CHAPTER THIRTEEN

THE GLOBAL GAME PLAN

*"This country reminds me of the substitute
football player who comes stumbling, ashen,
back to the bench and says, 'They're tackling
out there!' International sport is important to
every nation on this green earth. Of course
it's getting tougher."*

> Former Senator John Culver (D., Iowa),
> a member of the President's
> Commission on Olympic Sport

Few in Paris who watched AIA's dramatic win over
the Soviet national team on the day that Russian tanks
rolled into Afghanistan knew that a larger international athletic battle was already brewing. The battle
lines were drawn when leaders of some western
nations recommended athletics over tanks and
missiles as a means of reprisal.

Some argued that the 1980 Olympic boycott
would be a tremendous blow to the lofty principles of
the Olympic movement and demand unfair sacrifices
from innocent athletes who had trained for the Games.

Others, like *Newsweek's* Pete Axthelm, took the
opposite view. "To participate in the Games," he
wrote, "would be to legitimize a propaganda charade
and to help divert the world's attention from the
reality of Soviet aggression."[2]

Indeed, the Olympics carry the potential for
propaganda victories that overshadow athletic ones.
Held in billion dollar, specially-built complexes, each
time in a different corner of the world, and with a TV

audience of a billion-plus fans looking on, the pageantry of the modern Olympic Games makes the coronation of a king look third-rate, by comparison. It is the one event in which nations of the world can gather to showcase their strength while their armies remain at home.

During the 1980 boycott controversy *Newsweek* looked back at Olympic politics past. "Three times — in 1916, and 1940 and 1944 — the Games were cancelled by war. They have repeatedly fallen prey to international antagonisms: the new state of Israel was excluded in 1948 on a technicality under threat of an Arab boycott, and 28 African nations stayed away from Montreal in 1976 to protest New Zealand's rugby tour of South Africa."[3]

Others point out Hitler's use of the 1936 Berlin Games as a global stage to trumpet the glories of Nazism. The murder of eleven Israelis by Palestinian terrorists in Munich in 1972 provided the most tragic proof that the Olympics could not be insulated from real world politics.

Champion athletes can foster the belief that their nation is superior and correct in its policies. "The 1980 edition of the *Book of the Party Activist,* the bible of Soviet Communist Party members, noted that the 'decision . . . to hold the Olympic Games (in Moscow) has become convincing evidence of the . . . correctness of the foreign policy course of our country.' "[4]

The effort to influence extends beyond the Olympics into other facets of international sport. For example, when a Russian recently won the World Chess Championship he used his victory to cultivate the Soviet Union's political system by saying, "This proves once again that we have a better system."[5]

Nor is the approach limited to the Soviet Union.

Cuba is another country that has used athletics to further the ideals of its Communist dictator. When Fidel Castro took over, this small island nation was a nobody in the international athletic arena. Today, Cuba is a world power. Some of the more pessimistic onlookers believe the Cubans could soon overtake the United States in overall Olympic medals.

American citizens will get a close-up look at the rest of the world during the 1984 Olympics. Los Angeles, California is the site of the '84 Games. "Amateur sports will never receive as much attention in this country as it will during the Los Angeles Games," said F. Don Miller, U.S. Olympic Committee Executive Director. "If we fall on our face and the socialist countries triumph, it will be terribly discouraging."[6]

The United States has consistently lost ground in international competition in recent years and it is the Communist nations that are taking up the slack. In the 1976 Olympics, the United States finished third (unofficially, of course) behind the Soviet Union and East Germany, a nation of only 17 million people.

"We have a rebuilding job to do in the international arena," Miller told members of the Athletes in Action National Leadership Team during a private meeting at the Olympic headquarters. "The wounds must be repaired because they are cancerous."

The Communist nations put top priority on the development of their athletes, a primary reason for their international success. Since its first Olympic appearance at Helsinki in 1952, the Soviet Union has won nearly 1,000 medals — more than any other nation in the world during that time period.

What lies behind the Communist success? In the Soviet Union, editor Anatole Tchikovski of Moscow's *Physical Culture and Sports* estimates "the system" accounts for 99% of the country's international champions.

"The 'system' works like this: The constitution encourages the development of mass physical culture and sport (article 24) and guarantees the right of the people to take part (article 41).

"A special role is assigned to schools where physical training is a compulsory subject and the youths are graded the same way they are in reading and arithmetic."[7]

"The socialist countries really believe in early identification of athletes," Miller noted. "They conduct blood testing and body confirmation when kids are eight or 10 years old."[8]

"Those who excel in competition are sent to junior sport schools (JSS) or voluntary sports clubs (VSC). Training does not stop with graduation but continues, and sometimes intensifies, in school, factory, collective farm and army sport clubs. Russia has 220,000 of these clubs, located wherever people work or study."[9]

America's athletic power is threatened in basketball where it has traditionally been preeminent. Since basketball became an Olympic sport in 1936, the American men's team has played 70 games. It has compiled an amazing record of 69-1. The single loss was to the Russians after a controversial three seconds were added to the clock in the 1972 championship game.

Athletes in Action respects the power of Russia and other European teams. But many Americans don't. Coach Al McGuire, now a TV commentator, says, "Before, we've won with raw power and talent, but the rest of the world is catching up with us."

Lee Rose, coach at the University of South Florida, after directing the U.S.A. basketball team to a fifth-place finish in the Soviet-sponsored Spartakaide

Games, told an AP writer that the Soviet teams he coached against were "basically professional. The average age on our squad is 20, while the average on Moscow is 30 or 31."[10]

Soviet basketball players and athletes in other sports have every reason to continue competing as long as possible. But in the United States it does not pay to be a post-college athlete.

Here's why: The U.S. has historically drawn the backbone of its teams from the talent pool of the nation's colleges and universities and has been able to dominate many international events. In recent years, however, the young American athletes have lost their powerful grip on the rest of the world. "The problem, essentially," says Dave Hannah,"is that our 18-21-year-old college athletes can no longer compete with the 25-30-year-old Russian and eastern European athletes. The additional competing years available to the communist athlete give him opportunity to advance his strength and technique and give him a big edge in experience."

Such is not the case with promising American athletes, though during college each receives every opportunity to reach his potential. The finest facilities, competition and coaching are available; if he is injured, the best in rehabilitative equipment is at his disposal. He is fed, clothed and housed.

But after graduation day he no longer has his college coach. He must find a training facility, and more importantly, a job. He has a tough time finding quality international competition.

The President's Commission on Olympic Sport diagnosed other problems. In part, it concluded: "There are three basic modes of sports organizations employed by successful sporting nations. In one, government is in control. In another, a non-government sports authority is in control. In the third, no one is in control. Only the U.S. uses the third method."[11]

In recent years, however, there have been positive developments such as the centralization of some offices and training facilities in Colorado Springs. And the U.S. Olympic Committee has developed a number of outstanding programs, such as a corporate-involvement plan whereby an athlete's training regimen is integrated into his work schedule.

Athletes in Action has also proven an innovator. The athletic ministry is the only program in America whereby a post-college basketball player can continue to train full time, compete against top quality competition *and* retain his amateur status. America's international athletic future lies with the post-college athlete and with programs like Athletes in Action.

Under the direction of John Klein and Larry Amundson, AIA opened one of the nation's finest post-college training facilities in Fountain Valley, California in 1980. This Sports Center, which features, in part, a wrestling room and a gymnastics school, takes a unique approach: "We combine biblical training with athletic training," Amundson says.

Adds Hannah, "Beating the Russians may be great, but it's not worth it if our 12-year-old girls become nothing but athletic automatons. That's not beating the Russians — that's joining them." Indeed, AIA's goals would prohibit it from ever joining the Russians. The athletic ministry prefers to win souls more than games.

If winning games, however, means winning more to Christ, the AIA basketball team will be in the midst of the fight. The team has high aspirations for spiritual *and* athletic victories in the 1980's and beyond. Those aspirations may be realized if events that have already transpired in this decade are any indication.

One year after the win over the Russians in Paris, Athletes in Action was again chosen to represent the United States in Europe. This time it was the 12-team Philips World Invitation Club Basketball Championships in London, a tournament the U.S.A. had never won.

AIA went to London under the direction of a new head coach. Bill Oates had chosen to return to college coaching, citing a desire to travel less and spend more time at home with his family. After Jim Poteet served at the helm for a year, the job was placed in the capable hands of his assistant, Wardell Jeffries, in the spring of 1980.

The new coach got a surprise when he stepped off the airplane at London's Heathrow Airport — his team was seeded No. 1, and expected to reach the finals against number two seed and two-time defending champion Maccabi Tel Aviv of Israel. Israel is generally not considered an international basketball power, but Maccabi had imported talent from all over the world, including three former NBA players.

"We felt a responsibility to perform well," said Jeffries, "not only as Americans, but also as Christians." This was doubly important in the European tournament: AIA would not be permitted to present its usual halftime evangelistic program, so all the team's talking would be done on the court. And the trip to Europe provided a unique opportunity to disclaim a deeply-imbedded European stereotype about Christianity — that Christians are "sissies," in need of a crutch.

A *London Observer* writer mentioned the issue in his column: "You wouldn't expect them to be that good at basketball, with them being only, you know, Christians."

AIA had to win just twice to reach the finals, a

benefit of the No. 1 seeding. The American representative opened play against an English team from Don-
caster. Two things stood out about the game: the
narrowness of the American win (67-65 after a
second-half lapse), and, strangely enough, the referee,
who, everyone agreed, was a near-perfect double for
the late Peter Sellers, alias "Inspector Clouseau" in
the Pink Panther movie series. The referee seemed to
enjoy his identification with Clouseau, much to the
pleasure of the audience, even going out of his way to
mimic mannerisms of the "Inspector."

In its second game, AIA beat London's Crystal
Palace, the host team, 94-84, to move into the finals.
Maccabi Tel Aviv had meanwhile won both its en-
counters and the anticipated championship clash was
on.

The media hyped the "Christians-versus-Jews"
theme, and a capacity crowd jammed into the Crystal
Palace National Sports Centre. A group of Jewish
students, in London on overseas study programs, were
the most vocal fans in the audience, shrieking a
continuum of Hebrew chants. Before the game they
unfurled a large banner that read:

"AIA HAS THE SON
MACCABI HAS THE FATHER"

No one left the Crystal Palace disappointed. The
London Guardian called the play of Maccabi and AIA
"the highest standard of competitive basketball ever
seen in England."

At halftime, the teams had battled to a 50-50
stalemate. "Get your hands up under the boards,"
Eldon Lawyer, the new assistant coach, told the
players. "Make them work for everything they get."

Maccabi's massive Earl Williams did his share of
work; he was intimidating on the boards, and before
the game was two-thirds over had grabbed 12 re-

AIA's 177-pounder Don Shuler was the only American to earn a gold medal during the Soviet-sponsored Spartakaide Games (1979).

Tim Hall (50) takes a rebound from Earl Williams of Maccabi Tel Aviv in championship game of 1981 Philips World Invitaton Club Tournament in London.

Tim Hall shoots over Billy Paultz of Houston Rockets in a 1979 preseason exhibition game in San Clemente, Calif.

bounds. But his intimidation tactics didn't stop there.

"Every time you touch me, I'm gonna hit ya," he threatened Tim Hall who guarded him in AIA's man-to-man defense. Unfazed, the smaller Hall scrapped for nine rebounds of his own.

With less than a minute remaining, AIA clung tenaciously to a 92-90 lead. "You're not going to beat us, we're too good," Williams said to Hall over the deafening crowd noise. Just moments later, however, Williams was silenced in a dramatic way.

Twice in the game's final moments the hulking Maccabi forward stepped to the foul line with three chances to make two free throws. Both times he missed every attempt, any two of which would have tied the game. Two of his shots missed the entire backboard. Hall, Dan Frost and newer players Steve Schall, Gig Sims, Dave Johnson and L.A. Smith, were more successful in the clutch. Together they assured AIA's dramatic 96-92 win.

Hannah called the triumph "AIA's greatest tournament win ever." Adding icing to the sweet victory were comments like the one an Englishman made to Hall after the game. "Don't worry about not being able to give your program," he said. "Your response to the officials and your fair play said more than you could ever say here at halftime."

Besides, the sports media said it for them. English newspapers, with a combined circulation of over 11 million, carried stories about the "God Squad's" message, and the team appeared twice on "Grandstand" (the BBC's answer to "Wide World of Sports") where the audience ranged between five and seven million.

Dennis Cantrell, the former player and now team director, was besieged by representatives of many countries wanting AIA to visit. "Nothing," he said, "has opened more doors for our ministry than winning this tournament."

All of those doors were international ones, however, and in order to pass through those future portals, AIA first had to resolve a domestic crisis.

FOOTNOTES

1. Dave Burchett, "America's Amateur Plight: Is There an Answer?" *Athletes in Action*, 1978, p. 38, col. 1.
2. Pete Axthelm, Olympic Boycott, *Newsweek*, Jan. 28, 1980, p. 24.
3. Dennis A. Williams, "Olympic Politics Past," *Newsweek*, Jan 28, 1980, p. 24.
4. Allan J. Mayer, "National Affairs," *Newsweek*, Jan. 28, 1980, p.23.
5. Joe Smalley, "AIA and the Olympics," *Athletes in Action*, Fall 1979, p. 40, col. 1.
6. Kenneth Reich, "Olympic Training," *Los Angeles Times*, Feb. 24, 1981, part I, p. 7, col. 2.
7. Bill Shirley, "The Soviet System," *Los Angeles Times*.
8. Ibid.
9. Ibid.
10. David Minthorn, "Basketball Coach Wants Olympic Strategy Set Early," *Register*, Aug. 5, 1979, p. D5, col. 3.
11. Dave Burchett, "America's Plight: Is There An Answer?", *Athletes in Action*, 1978, p. 38, col. 1.

FUTURE TENSE

*"I am more interested in the future than the
past, for that is where I expect to spend the
rest of my life."*

A lot of people were making it tough for AIA to
stay in southern California.

In Los Angeles, there were Kings and Lakers,
Bruins and Trojans; nearly a score more were farther
south . . . even the Angels figured against them. Could
AIA continue to "ram," or at best, "dodger" the
competition? Especially when the competition included
the Pacific Ocean and Sea World, Hollywood glitter
and Universal Studio tours, surfing, roller-skating
championships, you name it. It was an uphill battle —
who dared take on Mickey Mouse, anyway?

AIA had dared. And AIA had succeeded, beaten
the odds. Its home-game attendance was at one time
second only to UCLA among amateur basketball
teams in California. AIA had proven it could handle
the competition; but its home games had nevertheless
proven a no-win situation.

It cost substantial sums to fly opponents from
eastern and mid-western states all the way to California. And if playing meant interrupting conference
schedules, universities insisted on even higher
guarantees.

When AIA did not consistently bring in top-ranked teams from different regions, attendance began to slip, especially among fans whom AIA most wanted to reach — the non-churched population. Bringing opponents to California was expensive, but traveling cross-country *to* the competition cost even more.

Athletes in Action was not alone. Even heavily-capitalized professional sports leagues were realigning their divisions geographically to cut travel expenses as fuel costs soared. Every college in the land was feeling the same pinch. And a pinch to a large state-financed university translates to a major squeeze for a faith-run ministry. Something had to be done.

Hannah half-jokingly suggested what later proved to be the solution. He and Cantrell were conducting some business in Memphis, Tenn. "Why don't we just move the team here?" Hannah said.

"Sounds good to me," Cantrell replied, without giving it much thought. Cantrell later gave it thought, however, and the idea excited him. After a six-month study of the Memphis area, Hannah was excited too.

The situation looked ideal: if Atlanta is the hub of the South and Dallas of the Southwest, Memphis is certainly the hub of the Mid-South. The location would put the team near universities in the South-eastern, Metro, and Big Ten conferences. "We should save between 30 and 40 percent on travel costs," Cantrell concluded after conducting a comprehensive financial study.

Hannah, after several trips to the city, observed another inherent advantage. "People love basketball here," he noted. They (Memphis State University) sell out every game at the (Mid-South) coliseum (10,000 seats)."

Though AIA's other teams would remain in Fountain Valley, the basketball squad would take its future shots in Memphis, Tennessee. The move was announced at a May 29, 1981 press conference in Memphis.

"I'm delighted," responded C. Tiffany Bingham, Jr., Executive Vice President of the Memphis Chamber of Commerce. "It's a super basketball city. They'll have a substantial impact."

Gordon Sprague, Director of the Memphis Parks and Recreation Department, added, "Having a quality program like Athletes in Action in Memphis opens up a whole new facet of recreation and entertainment."

That's part of what Athletes in Action hopes to accomplish through community involvement, speaking opportunities, home games, clinics and summer camps.

Cantrell and Hannah see even greater potential. "The real impact," Cantrell says, "comes in leading people to Christ and watching Him change lives. That's an impact with eternal consequences."

Though Memphis is home, AIA will continue to visit as many as 50 cities a year. This team belongs on the road, to minister wherever God opens doors.

And the ministry continues to multiply. Athletes in Action has launched a new five-minute nationwide radio show. A half-hour sports magazine TV show is in the works. The players hope for another crack at the World Championships. And Coach Jeffries' goal is to "place several of our players on the next U.S. Olympic team."

The players that God chooses and uses change, but their message remains the same. And the ministries of those He has used continue elsewhere . . .

*Tim Hall** is attending Denver Baptist Bible College and Seminary in Denver, Colorado, where he now applies his intense approach in a study for the pastorate.

*Irv Kiffin is playing basketball in Europe and has a ministry with the numerous other American players in the European leagues.

*Ralph Drollinger, after fulfilling his four-year commitment to AIA, finally decided to go pro in 1980. A year later, however, after knee problems plagued him with the Dallas Mavericks, he elected to give all his professional bonus money and salary to the Campus Crusade International fund to help reach people for Christ. He and Karen have since raised their missionary support and rejoined Campus Crusade staff, where they attend the International School of Theology.

*Brad and Becky Hoffman live near Sacramento, California where Brad helps manage a dairy. Both are enjoying their son Nate; Brad does some speaking and serves Christ through his local church. He plays a little church league ball, and his old teammates still kid him about being too short and too slow.

*Dave Hannah continues to lead the charge, to fight the fight of faith. He and AIA have lost some battles, taken their lumps — but in Christ, they're winning the war.

There is a cost for commitment. Sacrifices, like the money Ralph Drollinger chose to forego, have been made. Other players have turned down lucrative business opportunities. But whatever the sacrifice, there's no reason for regret. As Drollinger says, "You can either spend your life or invest it."

Hannah agrees. "The greatest use of life," he says, "is to spend it for something that will outlast it."

The principle applies to the collective talents of the Athletes in Action team. When other teams play, the results count for the scorebook and conference standings. But AIA's results count for eternity. When AIA plays, it's more than a game.

For basketball information, write:

> Athletes in Action USA Basketball
> 3648 Win Place
> Memphis, TN 38115

or call: (901) 795-4084.

Send $3.50 for the current copy of the AIA USA Basketball Yearbook.